INDONESIA

TIME-LIFE BOOKS/AMSTERDAM

COOKERY AROUND THE WORLD

INDONESIA

KUSUMA WIDJAYA / ROLAND MARSKE

Recipe photographs: Foodphotography Eising

Thailand

South China Sea

Philippines

Malaysia

Pacific Ocean

Malay Peninsula

Brunei

Sabah

Celebes Sea

Lake Toba

Sarawak

BORNEO

Sumatra

Singapore

MOLUCCAS

Padang

Kalimantan

Sulawesi

Irian Jaya

Indian Ocean

Jakarta

Madura

LESSER SUNDA ISLANDS

Java

Bali

Flores

Lombok

Sumbawa

Timor

Sumba

0   450km

CONTENTS

Indonesia: A Nation of Islands ——————————— 6

A Living Tradition ——————————————— 9
   The Torajas of Sulawesi ————————————— 10
   The Bataks of Sumatra ——————————————— 10
   The Dayaks of Kalimantan —————————————— 11
   Civilization from Distant Shores ————————— 12
   Shadow Plays ——————————————————— 13
   Islam in Indonesia ————————————————— 14
   Hinduism on Bali —————————————————— 14
   Colonial Rule and Independence ————————— 15
   Indonesian Cuisine ————————————————— 16
   The Foreign Contribution —————————————— 16
   A Wealth of Spices ————————————————— 17
   The Culinary Traditions of the Islands —————— 18
   Restaurants and Eating Places —————————— 20
   Mobile Snack Bars ————————————————— 20
   The Daily Menu ——————————————————— 22
   Thirst-quenchers and Other Drinks ——————— 24

Recipes ——————————————————————— 27
   Rice ——————————————————————————— 27
   Sambals and Curries ———————————————— 41
   Meat, Poultry and Fish ——————————————— 65
   Vegetables and Tofu ———————————————— 95
   Desserts ——————————————————————— 123

Suggested Menus ——————————————————— 138
Glossary —————————————————————————— 140
Recipe Index ———————————————————————— 142
Acknowledgements ————————————————————— 144

INDONESIA: A NATION OF ISLANDS

Java, Bali, Borneo, Sumatra—the very words conjure up images of glorious sandy beaches and dense rainforests, of coconut palms and lush terraced rice fields, of colourful tribal rituals and an idyllic tropical lifestyle. Over 13,000 islands make up the equatorial archipelago of Indonesia, islands remarkable not only for their great beauty, but for their ethnic diversity and rich cultural heritage. Foreigners have long been drawn to Indonesia's shores, from hostile traders lured by dreams of exploiting its abundant natural treasures, to missionaries in search of converts and peaceful travellers looking for a paradisiacal retreat. The Indonesians, for their part, have always been open to these outside influences, embracing the mores of each successive wave of invaders and absorbing them into their native culture. The evidence for this blending of cultures is to be found everywhere: ancient tribal rites and beliefs in the supernatural mingle with elements from all the world's great religions; in Sulawesi, Portuguese boat-building techniques and designs are still adhered to; and the Indonesian language is sprinkled with words that are a lasting reminder of Dutch rule.

The combination of a fascinating, complex history and stunning tropical landscape make Indonesia a tourists' haven. One of the delights awaiting the traveller is the food, which is recognized as being among the finest Asia has to offer. Despite enduring centuries of European domination, Indonesians have always held fast to their native style of cooking. Inspired by their myriad exotic spices and abundant variety of regional produce, they have created a memorable cuisine that is characterized by a carefully balanced and contrasting mix of textures and flavours.

This book reflects the diversity of Indonesian cookery. The first chapter introduces the country itself, its geography, history, peoples and traditions. It describes the different cooking styles, and also provides information on local eating habits and regional specialities. Then follows a selection of authentic recipes drawn from all over Indonesia; these are grouped in sections according to the main ingredients, in no particular order as it is customary in Indonesia to bring all the dishes to the table at the same time.

Each recipe is illustrated by a colour photograph, and, where necessary, clear step-by-step pictures illustrate some of the more complicated techniques. Complementing the recipes are notes on some of the more important ingredients, and suggestions for variations. A short introduction to each chapter, together with information boxes, provide practical hints and details about typical regional produce, dishes and ingredients.

At the end of the book, a glossary defines some of the less familiar terms and ingredients used in Indonesian cookery, and suggested menus enable you to re-create the feel and flavours of an Indonesian meal at your own table. So, enjoy the food of Indonesia—*Salamat makan!*

A LIVING TRADITION

The archipelago of Indonesia, the world's largest collection of islands, is strung out through the Pacific and Indian oceans in a broad arc bridging the continents of mainland Asia and Australia. While over half of these islands, being little more than rocks protruding from the water, have no name, and all but about a thousand are uninhabited, their total land mass is almost eight times that of the United Kingdom. If the surface area of the surrounding seas is taken into account, then Indonesia occupies an area the size of Europe—from Ireland to the Urals, and from Helsinki to Sicily. So immense is this island group, that when the morning sun breaks over the highlands of Irian Jaya (western New Guinea) at the eastern end, in Sumatra, in the far west, it is still the middle of the night.

The diversity of this huge and fragmented nation is reflected in its beautiful and dramatic landscape, where impenetrable rainforests and active volcanoes provide a striking backdrop to tiny coral atolls, coastal swamps, lush terraced paddy fields and palm-fringed tropical beaches. However, despite being blessed with such vast natural resources—for example, the mineral-rich volcanic soil is among the most fertile in the world— Indonesia remains a Third World country, with most of the population living below the poverty line.

The lives of Indonesia's inhabitants have, to a very great extent, been dictated by their country's island structure, in which the seas and mountains have served as natural barriers, preserving and reinforcing ethnic, cultural and regional differences. More than 350 ethnic groups, many of whom still retain a distinct cultural identity, speak between them some 250 regional languages and a range of dialects, as well as *Bahasa Indonesia*, which was formally adopted as the national language in 1945.

Anthropologists are unsure of the origins of the first-known migrants into Indonesia, who arrived some 30,000 years ago. The ancestors of the present-day Malay peoples of Indonesia—who make up the majority of the country's 170 million inhabitants—migrated in two great waves from the mainland of Southeast Asia. The first were the culturally retarded, neolithic Proto-Malays, who withdrew into the remote uplands on the arrival of the second group, the Deutero-Malays, who brought with them a more advanced Bronze-Age civilization and settled in the coastal areas. These early peoples are represented today by such diverse groups as the Torajas, Bataks and Dayaks who, thanks to their isolation, have succeeded in preserving through many generations their ancestors ancient customs and traditions.

The Torajas of Sulawesi

The rugged, beautiful highland region around Makale and Rantepao in southern Sulawesi is the homeland of around 350,000 Torajas, once among the most remote peoples in Indonesia. Particularly remarkable are their richly carved and decorated traditional dwellings, with sweeping saddle-shaped roofs that resemble buffalo horns.

Although many of the Torajas' ancient rites and beliefs have died out, or have been watered down over the centuries as the community has come under the influence of both Christianity and Islam, ancestral ceremonies still form an integral part of their day-to-day existence. Death is a focal point, but more as a cause for celebration than mourning. There is a strong belief that in the afterlife the souls of the dead travel to Puya, a peaceful, harmonious land where spirits lead untroubled lives. If, however, a soul cannot gain admission to Puya, it is destined to become a homeless, evil spirit, free to intervene in the lives of the living,

inflicting disease or crop failure. In order to guarantee the entry of souls to Puya, the Torajas stage elaborate Feasts of the Dead, which are held each year after the rice harvest. These joyous and lavish proceedings, which take place in addition to the simpler ceremonies that follow the death itself, climax in the mass slaughter of water buffaloes, whose spirits accompany the dead on their journey and ensure their safe passage, Following burial, ritual sacrifices must be made to the dead, who are represented by life-sized, carved wooden effigies (*tau-tau*). These symbolic figures are posted on wooden balconies before the cliffside graves, their outstretched arms a constant reminder to members of their families of the need for sacrifices.

The Bataks of Sumatra

Around the shores of Lake Toba, amid the splendid scenery of northern Sumatra, live the Bataks, a grouping of once fierce and warlike clans whose existence, until the late 19th century, was largely an isolated one. Within the strongly patriarchal Batak society, the male offspring play a central role, their prayers an essential offering in ensuring eternal peace for the souls of their dead parents. In some clans, for those who die childless, a life-sized wooden puppet (*si gale gale*) representing a male child is made to perform a grotesque dance to music during funerary rituals.

According to legend, the first *si gale gale* was created in a village where the chief's son had died. The chief was overcome by grief, not only for his son,

In the mountainous Batak country, and on the island of Samosir in Lake Toba, many Batak tribes still live in communal dwelling houses, richly decorated with mosaics and woodcarvings.

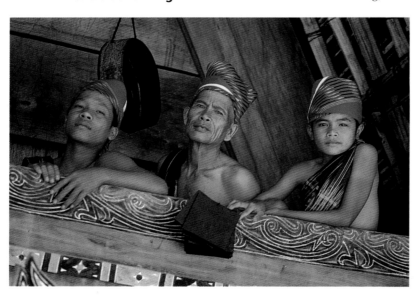

but also for the subsequent fate of his own soul. To console their chief, and to restore his peace of mind, the villagers fashioned a symbolic representation of his son in the form of a wooden puppet.

The Dayaks of Kalimantan

The Dayaks, natives of Kalimantan in Borneo, inhabit a remote interior region that is accessible only by river. Instantly recognizable by their pierced, elongated earlobes and their intricate body tattoos, they are descended from headhunting warriors, for whom this macabre pursuit was not only a manifestation of personal prestige and masculinity, but a practice with deep spiritual significance. When an enemy was decapitated, his strength was transferred to the victor's tribe. The severed heads, cured by smoking over

a fire, were accorded a special respect, because the dead were thought to be closer to the gods than the living.

As recently as the beginning of the 20th century, headhunters were still a much-feared race. In 1945 these fears were realized when Dayaks captured members of the Japanese occupation forces who had unwittingly strayed into their territory. Today, the only visible reminders of those turbulent times are the ancient headdresses of the elders, and their dwellings—great long houses built on wooden piles and housing up to 50 families. In the past, when villages were under constant threat of attack from rival tribes, a long house was far easier to defend than a scattered gathering of huts. This communal lifestyle still persists in many parts of Borneo, for it allows groups of children, or the community's sick and elderly, to be more easily cared for.

Lush vegetation flourishes under the equatorial sun of northern Sumatra. In the steamy rainforests of this wild and rugged island, the fifth largest in the world, trees grow to heights of 60 metres or more.

Kenikmatan kretek filter dengan cita rasa sempurna

Ancient meets modern in Lombok. Kretek cigarettes, sweetened with cloves, are Indonesia's most popular brand of tobacco.

A Balinese craftsman carefully applies the gilding to a three-dimensional carved wooden puppet,

Civilization from Distant Shores

The history of Indonesia is one of many distinct and separated regions, of successive waves of immigrants, invaders and traders, all of whom have left a mark on the islands' culture. Religious influence, too—Hinduism, Buddhism, Islam, Christianity—played a key role in the development of a unique national identity at a time when Europe was still immersed in the Middle Ages. The legacy of these centuries of subtly interwoven cultural styles and beliefs is much in evidence today, not least in the rich architectural remains of Java. From the 8th to 10th centuries AD, vast temple complexes were built here; Borobudur, in central Java, is one of the world's largest and finest Buddhist monuments.

Shadow Plays

Indonesia has a thriving Hindu heritage which permeates the country's crafts, folklore and dramatic arts. A foremost example is the *wayang kulit*, or shadow play, found all over Bali and Java. The original purpose of these plays, which are full of symbolism, was to drive away evil spirits and to make contact with dead ancestors. The storyteller and puppet master, known as a *dalang*, picked up messages from the spirit world and relayed them, through the medium of the puppets, to the living. As Hinduism spread, the puppets were increasingly used to act out tales from the Ramayana, a Sanskrit epic poem comparable to the Odyssey or the Iliad. The popularity of these performances gradually led to the establishment of travelling shadow theatres.

The elaborately painted puppets are fashioned from flat, cut-out pieces of buffalo hide or goatskin attached to a wooden rod. During the performance, the *dalang* sits cross-legged behind a white canvas screen. A lamp placed above him lights the puppets from behind, casting their shadows onto the screen. The puppets—"goodies" on the right and "baddies" on the left—are manipulated by the *dalang*, who uses different voices and different modes of speech, from popular to courtly or ceremonial language, to recount stories from Indian history and mythology.

As the narrator speaks, his fingers operate the puppets, while his feet work a metal rattle whose sound lends emphasis to particularly dramatic moments in the tale. Dialogue between characters is separated by the hollow thump of a wooden hammer, also wielded by the *dalang*. The performance is accompanied by a percussion-type orchestra, or *gamelan*, and sometimes also a chorus of female singers. The audience was originally segregated according to gender, the men sitting on the *dalang*'s side, where they could see the highly decorated puppets and the orchestra, and the women behind the screen, seeing only the shadows.

In the flickering glow of a burning oil lamp, which symbolizes the Sun, the dalang and his dancing puppets bring to life the ancient Hindu legends.

A Hindu priest

Stunning mountain scenery provides a spectacular backdrop for the Bukittinggi mosque (top) in western Sumatra, and the distinctive peaked roofs of traditional Minangkabau dwellings.

Islam in Indonesia

For about 90 per cent of the population of Indonesia the dominant religion is Islam, which was introduced during the 13th century by Muslim traders from southern India, establishing the country as the world's most easterly outpost of Islam. By the 15th century, Muslim kingdoms were to be found on Java and other larger islands on the main trading route. Indonesian Islam today is a unique blending of doctrines that has evolved to suit the needs and aspirations of the islanders. Ritual ceremonies and the worship of traditional ancestral spirits exist in harmony with the tenets of all the three main religions of Hinduism, Buddhism and Islam. Only those peoples living in the remote and inaccessible inland areas escaped the influence of the new religion, which first took hold in coastal areas. One such group are the

Tenggerese, who live in the mountains around Java's Mount Bromo, a volcano that is one of Indonesia's most stunning natural features. Their religion is a blend of Hinduism and Buddhism.

Hinduism on Bali

Though the tiny, paradise-like island of Bali is situated only two kilometres from Java, the islanders resisted the spread of Islam, developing instead a unique and complex form of Hinduism practised today by 95 per cent of the population. Central to Balinese Hinduism, which has its own highly theatrical customs and ceremonies, is a belief in the immortality of the soul; man's existence is seen as a perpetual cycle of rebirths.

This belief in reincarnation means that death is not seen as a sad event, but rather as an occasion for joyous celebration. Funerals, known as *ngaben*s, are splendidly colourful occasions, and villagers will often stage mass cremations in order to spread the cost of the lavish ceremonies. The body (which is exhumed if it has aready been buried once) is carried in procession to the funeral pyre on top of a 12-metre-high wood and bamboo tower decorated with coloured paper, tinsel, mirrors, flowers and silk. During the journey, the mourners endeavour to shake off any evil spirits which may be pursuing the deceased by swiftly twirling the tower around on its axis whenever they reach a crossroads. When they arrive at the burial ground, the body is placed on the pyre and set alight. The *ngaben* ends with the ashes being collected and taken on a litter to the sea, where they are then cast onto the waters, freeing the soul.

Colonial Rule and Independence

The first Europeans to find their way to Indonesia were Portuguese traders, who arrived at the beginning of the 16th century. Once there, they exploited whatever commodities they came across—slaves, spices, gold and ivory.

Scarcely a hundred years later, however, they were overthrown by the Dutch, victors in the fight for the lucrative spice trade. The Dutch then set about protecting their interests by establishing trading posts across the region that comprises present-day Indonesia. By the 17th century they held sway over huge amounts of territory, laying the foundations of a powerful commercial empire.

The period of Dutch colonial rule ended with the Japanese occupation during World War II, and on 17 August 1945, Indonesia was proclaimed a republic. The Dutch returned, however, and attempted to rebuild their former empire. Freedom was only secured at the end of 1949 after a long and bloody conflict. In 1967 President Achmed Sukarno was ousted in an abortive Communist coup and was replaced by General Suharto; in the anti-Communist witch-hunt that followed, an estimated one million people were murdered in the name of freedom.

Many of the victims of this massacre were Chinese. First brought to the islands as workers by the Dutch during colonial times, the Chinese population in Indonesia today numbers some four million people and constitutes one of the country's most important ethnic minorities. The diligence and enterprise of the community have secured its members influential positions in every sector of the economy. Although some Chinese have become thoroughly Indonesianized, during the 20th century their wealth and business skills have been envied and resented by many Indonesians, and the community has suffered both social and physical oppression as a consequence.

In Indonesia's capital Jakarta, "city of a million villages", East meets West in a fascinating collision of the modern and the traditional.

Dressed in an ornate costume adorned with fresh flowers, a Balinese performs a ritual dance, an activity that is still largely a male preserve in Indonesia.

The gleaming peeled roots of the cassava plant, source of tapioca starch.

In her primitive roadside kitchen, powered by gas cylinder, a woman prepares banana fritters, a popular Balinese snack.

Indonesian Cuisine

Indonesia's national motto, "Unity in Diversity", is one that can be applied to many aspects of the country's culture, not least its cuisine. To those travellers who eat only in their hotels, without endeavouring to seek out smaller, local restaurants, there may at first glance appear to be little choice. For whether you are eating in western Sumatra or eastern Nusa Tenggara, the dishes on offer can look very similar; popular and familiar dishes such as fried rice (*nasi goreng*) or the Indonesian version of chop suey (*cap cay goreng*) are available everywhere. If, however, you are willing to venture farther afield in search of interesting culinary experiences, and allow yourself to be tempted by the little food stalls or travelling kitchens found in every street, you will find that the variety so characteristic of traditional Indonesian cuisine is not confined to home cooking but can, with a little effort, be sampled easily and cheaply.

The Foreign Contribution

Throughout its long history as a trading country, Indonesia has been exposed to prolonged and numerous foreign influences, among them Indian, Arabian, Portuguese, Dutch, English and Chinese. The national cuisine— regarded as one of the finest in Asia— reflects this cosmopolitan past. Over the centuries, styles of cooking have overlapped and intermingled, creating today's unique variety of flavour and presentation.

From India came curries and the liberal use of spices, which Indonesia possesses in abundance. The Islamic influence is unmistakable in the popular technique of charcoal grilling small pieces of meat, known in Indonesia as *satay*. The incomparable flavour of the Indonesian satay—so different from the Arab *shish kebab* or the Caucasian *shashlik*—is achieved by first marinating the meat in *kecap manis* (sweet soy sauce), and serving it accompanied by a tangy peanut sauce.

Islam has a range of strict dietary rules which have also dictated culinary traditions in certain areas. For example, no Indonesian Muslim will eat pork (*babi*); only the Balinese, Chinese, Christians and other non-Muslim tribes in the highland regions include this meat in their diets. Another legacy of the Muslim influence is the relative scarcity of alcoholic drinks—although in the towns and cities they can be bought from the Chinese. During Ramadan, the annual month-long fast observed by the Islamic population, the faithful are not allowed to eat or drink anything from sunrise to sunset. At these times, it is the Chinese

community who comes to the rescue of unwitting hungry travellers!

The Chinese contribution to the cuisine of Indonesia is unmistakable. In fact, the utensils used in Indonesia are very similar to those found in Chinese kitchens. All the equipment needed for cooking Indonesian food is a *kuali* or *wajan*, a large, dome-shaped metal pan similar to the Chinese wok, a pestle and mortar—or an electric blender—for grinding spices and peanuts, and a large pot for cooking the rice.

The Dutch, during their centuries of colonial rule, contributed many European touches to local eating habits. Conversely, the flavourings of Indonesian cuisine spiced up some traditional Dutch dishes. It was the Dutch who brought back to Europe the famous *rijsttafel*, or "rice table", a tradition that dates back to the days of the spice trade, when the ruling Dutch held sumptuous banquets that were as much about entertainment as they were about eating. Tables, decorated with flowers, were loaded by waiters with bowls of rice and a carefully balanced and contrasting sequence of meat, fish or vegetable dishes and highly seasoned *sambals*. Today, this type of meal is usually served buffet-style.

Rijsttafel, at its most elaborate, epitomizes the variety and splendour of bonafide Indonesian cuisine. In the classic version, the entire meal is brought to the table at the same time—a European innovation. It usually consists of between 20 and 30 different dishes, with rice providing the focal point. Guest help themselves to a generous serving of fluffy rice and then, one by one—never at the same time—try a little from each of the dishes.

A Wealth of Spices

Indonesian cuisine is enriched by an enormous variety of exotic ingredients, in particular the many spices for which the archipelago is famed. For centuries, spice cultivation has been vital to the country's economy, and the cause of lengthy battles waged between the great European powers for control of the lucrative spice trade.

The following fresh and dry spices are all found in Indonesian cuisine, subtly blended to create an array of deliciously aromatic and richly coloured dishes: chili (*lombok*), cloves (*cengkeh*), lemon grass (*seré*), nutmeg (*pala*), tamarind (*asam java*), pepper (*merica*), ginger (*jahe*), galangal (*laos*), coriander (*ketumbar*), cinnamon (*kayu manis*), cardamon (*kepulaga*), garlic (*bawang puteh*) and shallots (*bawang*). Other popular flavouring ingredients are sweet soy sauce (*kecap manis*), chili sauce (*sambal*), shrimp paste (*terasi*), ground peanuts (*kacang*) and lime or lemon juice. Coconut juice (*santen*) is frequently substituted for milk, which is virtually unknown in Indonesian cookery; it gives a sweet and nutty flavour to dishes.

Shoppers at a Lombok market pick over the flat woven baskets filled with chili peppers, dried fish, nuts and spices—the glories of Indonesian cuisine.

At a roadside in Bima, in eastern Sumbawa, a woman arranges her colourful produce so as to catch the shopper's eye. The woven cloth of her sarong is batik, a traditional decorating technique in which wax or a starchy paste is used to resist colouring dyes.

The Cuisine of the Islands

The cuisine of Indonesia is notable for its great regional diversity; from island to island across the archipelago, the recipes and ingredients vary according to tradition, cultural preference, climate and availibility of foodstuffs, as well as religious belief—pork is never found in Muslim areas, for example.

As each island has its distinct ethnic groups, so it enjoys a subtly different cuisine from that of its neighbours.

The fervently Muslim Minangkabau, a matriarchal society whose homeland is in western Sumatra, is renowned for the excellence of its chefs, whose culinary skills are famous throughout Indonesia. Their delicious style of cooking is held to epitomize traditional Indonesian cuisine, and it can be sampled in specialized restaurants bearing the name *rumah makan padang* (after Padang, Sumatra's largest city). The dishes—often displayed in the restaurants' windows or laid out on the counter—mostly comprise meat, fish, vegetable and egg curries. These are accompanied by the obligatory large quantities of rice, which complements or is complemented by all traditional

Indonesian food. The majority of dishes are very spicy, due mainly to the large quantities of chili added to prevent unrefrigerated food from going off. To savour this tastiest of Indonesian cuisines in a restaurant, simply say the phrase *mau makan* ("I should like to eat") to the waiter, and without further ado a whole assortment of dishes, sometimes as many as 20, will be brought to your table. You can then take your pick from the various bowls, and you will only be charged for what you eat. The delicious, thick sauces served with the meal are free, so take generous helpings of these! If you prefer a more filling—and cheaper—alternative, order *nasi campur* (mixed rice); you will then be served a plate of steamed rice accompanied by a standard mixture of fish, meat or vegetables piled on top.

In Javanese cookery, chilis are used more sparingly. Sauces are generally sweeter, though no less spicy or aromatic; a characteristic ingredient is coconut milk, which gives sauces a pleasantly creamy texture, and palm sugar (known as *gula jawa,* or Java sugar), which is added to both sweet and savoury dishes.

Balinese cuisine is colourful and varied and boasts a great array of delicacies and exotic ingredients not found elsewhere. Pigs are bred on the island, inspiring the creation of a number of dishes unique to Bali, such as the spectacular *babi guling* (roast stuffed suckling pig). Desserts, too, are a particular speciality. East of Bali, in the Lesser Sunda Islands, the food is comparatively plain and simple. The islands are situated at the drier periphery of the tropical monsoon area, where lush green vegetation gives way to bush and steppe. Less fertile soil means a less abundant supply of land-grown foodstuffs; consequently, fish dishes dominate the islanders' diet.

As might be expected of an island whose population embraces so many different ethnic groups, Sulawesi offers the traveller a wide assortment of culinary delights. The Bugis, who live in the southwest of the island, have always been a seafaring people, skilled in boatbuilding and sailing, and their diet is largely a fish- and seafood-based one. Every evening the long beach promenade at Ujung Pandang, the capital of Sulawesi, is crammed with rows of closely packed mobile food stalls grilling a variety of fish over open fires. If you are lucky enough to visit the "longest counter in the world", look out for Bugi specialities such as goldfish (*ikan mas*), barbecued squid (*cumi cumi*) or a soup made from buffalo innards (*soto makassar*).

The cuisine enjoyed by the Torajas of southern Sulawesi is mainly vegetarian; only during the great Feasts of the Dead, when pigs and water buffaloes are freely slaughtered, does meat regularly appear on the menu. A typical dish is *pa'piong*, a mixture of meat and vegetables cooked inside a cut-off section of bamboo.

More exotic still is the cuisine of the Minahassa people, who live at the most northerly tip of Sulawesi. If you really hate the idea of eating dog—which necessity has rendered normal fare in this part of the world—take care when dining out in the local restaurants that you do not inadvertently order this peppery hot meat! Mice, bats and snakes may also feature on the menu.

Few tourists penetrate as far as the extreme east of Indonesia, to the Moluccas or beyond Irian Jaya (western New Guinea); consequently, the native cuisine is relatively little known. Staple starches here are tapioca, derived from the turnip-like root vegetable cassava, or manioc, and sago (*sagu*), which is extracted from the floury pith of the sago palm.

Harvesting rice in central Java. Over 40 per cent of this island's cultivated land is given over to intensive rice farming; the mineral-rich fertile soil can yield up to three crops a year.

At the Pasar Ikan market in Jakarta, a woman displays a neatly stacked pile of gleaming fish. Her sun hat, and the baskets in which the fish are carried, are made from plaited and woven grasses, an age-old craft practised throughout Indonesia by both men and women.

Restaurants and Eating Places

It is often said that Indonesians are more concerned about what they eat than where they eat it; the external appearance of a restaurant and its furniture or décor is of quite secondary importance when compared with the quality of the food itself. Even the humblest of eating houses is capable of turning out a feast fit for a king. There are various categories of eating place in Indonesia, ranging from superior air-conditioned *restoran*s, where menus are brought to the table and prices are correspondingly high, to simple little cafés known as *rumah makan*s, or "eating places". In the latter, the menu is usually shorter and written up on a board on the wall, or else the food is displayed in bowls and serving dishes under glass at the entrance.

When eating out in Indonesia there are a couple of basic rules to observe. Firstly, food is frequently served warm rather than hot. A request to have your meal heated up is likely to be met with bewilderment, for the Indonesians prefer not to eat their meals piping hot. Secondly, tipping serving staff is not customary in any restaurant.

Mobile Snack Bars

At nightfall, the busy streets, town squares and marketplaces throughout Indonesia play host to countless little

An itinerant vendor with his portable snack bar patiently waits to make a sale.

food stalls, or *warungs*, offering their freshly cooked wares to passers-by. Some of these makeshift stalls will comprise nothing more than a few planks, a piece of plastic sheeting and a couple of wooden stools. Others, mounted on tricycles or carts, are even more basic, but one thing they all have in common is that they seldom sell more than one speciality, which is advertized in large letters on the side of the stall or on a strip of cloth.

By going from one *warung* to the other, it is possible to put together a menu of contrasting courses. This way of eating also has the distinct advantage of allowing the customer to make any culinary requests directly to the cook; what's more, the delicious-smelling, mouthwatering dishes are prepared while you wait. From these traditional eating places, which cater to the tastes of the local population, you can be sure of getting tasty food and

excellent value for money.

Another characteristically Indonesian phenomenon are the travelling kitchens which ply the streets. The owner-chefs, who carry their utensils on a bicycle or handcart, or slung across their shoulders on a wobbly pole, will signal their arrival in a number of different ways, according to the delicacies on offer: the noodle-seller beats a frying pan with a spoon, while the soup vendor loudly thumps the handlebars of his bicycle with a wooden stick to persuade customers to sample his hot broth with meatballs.

Also not to be ignored are the many young children who make a living by selling food on the streets. Their little covered bins often conceal tasty morsels prepared by their mothers, so providing the more intrepid traveller with an easy—and cheap—means of sampling some authentic Indonesian home cooking.

At these cramped makeshift food stalls in Kalimantan, delicious filled pancakes are freshly made to order.

Stuffed pancakes and spring rolls (left) are prepared while you wait at this simple mobile snack bar.

Familiar and exotic fruit and vegetables, neatly arranged on mats and banana leaves, are spread for sale in a Borneo marketplace.

The Daily Menu

Many elderly Indonesians have experienced real hunger at some point in their lives, and even today the majority of households live relatively frugally. Rice, which is eaten up to three times a day, is more than just a staple starch, it is the very heart of the Indonesians' diet and shapes their way of eating. A bowl of rice serves as the focal point of a meal, the base around which all the other dishes are planned. Compared to the rice served in China or Japan, Indonesian rice is dry, less sticky and harder to pick up; when mixed with a sauce, however, it soaks up the liquid and can then, as is the custom in Indonesia, be scooped up with the fingers into little mouthfuls.

If you are the guest of an Indonesian family, the host will invite you to the table with the word *silakan* ("please"). Dishes are not served in any particular order but are usually brought to the table either all at once, or in quick succession, enabling each person to choose and combine dishes according to his preference and appetite. For European tastes, the portions of meat, fish or vegetables may seem rather small, but they are all designed to be accompanied by large quantities of rice—which also dilutes the impact of the fiery hot *sambals*! Once you have begun eating, you will continue to be served until you leave a small amount on your plate, thereby indicating that you have had enough. In Bali and Java, it is usual to leave a few grains of rice, a sign of gratitude to the gods.

Unlike the Chinese, the Indonesians do not eat from bowls, but from plates or banana leaves; the latter are very practical as they can just be thrown away afterwards. Fingers, rather than chopsticks, are used to pick up the food; it is customary, especially in rural areas, to eat with the fingers of the right hand as the left is regarded as "unclean". Most Indonesians today, however, are familiar with Western utensils, and use a spoon and fork. There is usually no need for a knife as anything that needs cutting up will have been dealt with beforehand by the cook.

Breakfast, lunch and dinner often consist of the same types of dishes, the only difference being the quantities. Dinner is traditionally a relaxed meal, enjoyed after sunset with family or friends. Those who can afford to do so load the table with delicious food. If some rice is left over, it can be fried the next day to make *nasi goreng*, delicious with a fried egg (*telor mata sapi*) on top or garnished with shredded omelette. Noodles (*bahmi*) provide a welcome alternative to rice, as does *gado gado*, a vegetable dish with a tangy peanut sauce.

All authentic Indonesian meals are made up of a selection of dishes with

contrasting flavours and textures. For every hot and spicy dish, a mild one is served; each sweet dish is balanced by something sour; and every fried one is offset by something steamed. As is the case in most tropical and subtropical countries, dessert will commonly consist of fresh fruit, which is available in abundance in Indonesia; everything from plump mangoes and creamy-white mangosteens, to juicy little rambutans and the delicious but foul-smelling king of fruits, the durian. Little cakes and tempting sweetmeats are enjoyed as between-meals snacks.

In contrast to the simplicity of this everyday fare, special occasions are celebrated with a ritual feast, or *slamatan*, a lavish banquet staged to ward off evil spirits and enlist the support of good ones. Any significant life event such as a birth, a death, a circumcision, or the start or completion of the building of a new house, is welcomed as an excuse for a *slamatan*.

Early in the morning on a Lombok beach, a group of young fishermen examine their day's haul. Indonesia, whose sea area is four times larger than its land area, boasts a staggering array of edible fresh fish.

Children eagerly queue at an ice juice stand to try one of Indonesia's many delicious fruit or coconut milk drinks.

Thirst-quenchers and Other Drinks

The Indonesians have a delicious and varied selection of natural drinks, both hot and cold. Many of these exotic-looking concoctions are made from coconut milk mixed with different fruits, or from finely crushed ice with brightly coloured scraps of gelatin; one such coconut-based drink, *bajigur*, is thickened with rice and sweetened with palm sugar. On street stalls you can buy sugar-cane juice (*air tebu*), squeezed straight into the glass, fresh coconut milk (*air kelapa*), citrus juices and a delicious avocado blend called *es*

pokat. Soft drinks such as Coca-Cola, Fanta and Sprite—the last often sold mixed with milk!—have now found their way to the most remote corners of the world. Indonesia has its own range of cheap and gaudily coloured soft drinks, but they are often very sweet.

Since the majority of Indonesians are Muslims, alcohol consumption across the country is relatively low; on islands where the inhabitants are followers of Islam, strong drink is forbidden. However, this only applies to products imported from the West, since the Indonesians are reluctant to give up their traditional home brews, such as *tuak*, a milky palm wine with a sweet-

On a stall in Yogyakarta, a woman deftly peels a pineapple for sale. The "eyes" of this fruit grow in a series of rows, and can easily be carved out to create this attractive spiral effect.

arak) or hot chocolate (*coklat panas*).

Beer (*bir*) is very popular with the tourists; the best-known brands are Beck's, Anker, Bintang (a Dutch beer), San Miguel and Guinness, also known as *bir hitam*, or "black beer". One should not assume, however, that these beers, brewed locally under licence, taste the same as the originals. Because few bars have refrigerators, beer is often served with ice cubes floating in it—consequently, the request *Tanpa es terimakasih* ("no ice, thank you!") soon becomes a vital addition to the tourist's repertoire!

About the only drink, apart from water (*air*), that Indonesians take with their meals is unsweetened weak tea (*teh*), which is drunk warm, or cold with ice cubes. Tea with sugar and milk is generally more expensive. Indonesia's thick, black, sweet coffee (*kopi*) is a powerful brew. First introduced by the Dutch in 1699, coffee has been cultivated since then in Sumatra, Sulawesi, Java and Bali. Many people roast and grind the beans themselves, sometimes mixing in roasted, ground peanuts, and then adding hot water to make the strong, freshly roasted brew, which is usually served in tall glasses.

and-sour flavour that is brewed for about a month. In the evenings, the locals gather in their favourite meeting places, known as *tempat tuak*s, to relax with their friends. Here, they sit around chatting, sipping *tuak*, and smoking *kretek*, a popular brand of clove-flavoured cigarettes.

The Balinese are very fond of their pink rice wine *brem*, made from glutinous rice with added coconut juice. Best served cold, it is deceptively mild-tasting but can be lethally potent, depending on its age. The rice brandy *arak* is distilled from *brem*. If taken straight, *arak* is barely drinkable, but it is delicious when added to coffee (*kopi*

RICE

I n common with most Asian cultures, rice is a major staple of Indonesian cooking. But unlike countries such as China or Thailand, where noodles also feature large on the menu, there is no substitute for rice in Indonesia and it appears on the table in various forms three times a day—breakfast, lunch and dinner.

The Indonesians cook rice in many different ways. The simplest, most general method—called *nasi putih*, or "white rice"—is by boiling long-grain white rice in water until all the liquid is absorbed and the rice is light and fluffy. This is served as a basic accompaniment to most dishes, from meat, fish and vegetables to spicy sambals and curries, and also soup. Other methods include cooking rice in coconut milk, frying it with different ingredients or wrapping glutinous rice in banana, palm or bamboo leaves.

Indonesia's best-loved national rice dish is *nasi goreng*. It consists of precooked rice fried with seasonings and a variety of ingredients such as shredded meat, fish, chicken, bean sprouts, mussels or shrimps, topped with a fried egg or shredded omelette.

However, as with European cuisine, it is often the least complicated dishes that show the greatest divergence of quality and flavour, according to the talent of the cook; and simple rice dishes, such as yellow rice, *nasi kuning*, and coconut rice, *nasi uduk*, are traditionally served at family or religious festive occasions.

Steamed rice

Simple · Basic recipe

Nasi putih

Serves 4

300 g long-grain rice

Preparation time: 35 minutes

1,100 kJ/260 calories per portion

1 Wash the rice until the water runs clear, then drain.

2 If you don't have an electric rice steamer, place the rice and ½ litre water in a heavy saucepan with a tight-fitting lid. Bring to the boil, then reduce the heat to very low and continue to cook the rice, covered, for 15 to 20 minutes. When all the water has been absorbed and the surface of the rice is dry, remove the pan from the heat. Keep the lid on the pan and leave the rice to stand for about 10 minutes before serving.

Notes: This method of boiling rice is usually referred to as "steamed". Indonesians mainly use husked rice. However, while polished white rice looks more attractive and keeps up to three years, it contains fewer vitamins and minerals and less fibre. The best long-grain rice includes Indonesian long-grain, Thai fragrant and basmati.

Indonesian cooks prefer to cook rice without salt. To suit European tastes, we suggest the addition of ½ tsp salt to the cooking water. To keep rice warm or reheat it, you can steam it in a sieve over boiling water.

Yellow rice

Simple · Java and Bali

Nasi kuning

Serves 4

300 g long-grain rice
2 curry leaves or bay leaves
½ tsp ground turmeric
¾ tsp ground coriander
¼ tsp ground cinnamon
¼ tsp ground cloves
salt
crispy fried onion rings (optional ·
see recipe, right)

Preparation time: 35 minutes

1,100 kJ/260 calories per portion

1 Wash the rice until the water runs clear, then drain.

2 Place the rice and ½ litre water in a heavy saucepan with a tight-fitting lid and add the spices. Bring to the boil, then reduce the heat to very low, stir the rice twice, so that the spices are evenly distributed, and cook, covered, for 15 to 20 minutes. When all the water has been absorbed and the surface of the rice is dry, remove the pan from the heat. Keep the lid on the pan and leave the rice to stand for about 10 minutes. Remove the curry or bay leaves and serve garnished, if you like, with crispy fried onion rings.

Crispy fried onion rings
Peel 8 shallots and cut them into very thin rings. Heat 4 tbsp oil in a frying pan over medium heat and brown the onion rings. Drain them on kitchen paper, leave to cool, then store in an airtight container until ready to use.

Variation:
Yellow coconut rice (*Nasi lemak*)
Instead of boiling the rice in water, use a similar quantity of coconut milk. Garnish with crispy fried onion rings.

Note: *Nasi kuning* is served in Indonesia on religious feast days.

Coconut rice

Nasi uduk

Simple • Java and Bali

Serves 4

**300 g long-grain rice
60 cl canned unsweetened
coconut milk
salt**

Preparation time: 35 minutes

3,900 kJ/930 calories per portion

1 Wash the rice until the water runs clear, then drain.

2 Place the rice, coconut milk and a little salt in a heavy saucepan with a tight-fitting lid and bring to the boil. As soon as the coconut milk comes to the boil, reduce the heat to very low and continue to cook the rice, covered, for 15 to 20 minutes. When all the liquid has been absorbed and the surface of the rice is dry, remove the pan from the heat. Keeping the lid on the pan, leave the rice to stand for about 10 minutes.

Note: Before using canned coconut milk, stir it thoroughly because during storage the cream rises to the top. If using compressed creamed coconut, mix it with hot water following the instructions on the packet. Once opened, or reconstituted, coconut milk does not keep well and should be used within 24 hours.

Coconut

The coconut palms of Indonesia are thought to have originated in the Pacific islands of Melanesia. Coconuts that fell into the sea floated thousands of kilometres across the water and were washed ashore on the Indonesian coast, where they began to sprout. Today, coconut products are one of Indonesia's major export industries.

Coconuts ripen in bunches 30 metres above ground, beneath a crown of feather-like leaves. The edible white kernel has three protective layers: a leathery outer skin, a fibrous husk between 4 and 6 cm thick and a hard brown shell.

Indonesians claim that coconuts have as many uses as there are days

in the year. Raw coconut is delicious to eat and the cavity liquid makes a refreshing drink; desiccated coconut is used in cakes or sweets; grated coconut is made into coconut milk, which can be bought in cans or in compressed blocks of creamed coconut that can be reconstituted with water.

The flesh is also processed into oil

and coconut butter. Apart from its culinary role, the oil is used in a wide variety of products, from soaps and shampoos to natural weedkiller and hydraulic brake fluid. The fibrous husk is processed into coir which is made into rope and matting, and the palm leaves are used for thatching and basketry.

Special fried rice

A little more complex • National dish **Nasi goreng istimewa** **Serves 4**

200 g long-grain rice

salt

250 g beef fillet or boned chicken

4 shallots

2 garlic cloves

¼ tsp terasi (see page 96)

100 g Chinese cabbage

1 large carrot

100 g bean sprouts

200 g peeled, cooked shrimps
or prawns

3 to 4 tbsp coconut or vegetable oil

100 g shelled fresh, or frozen, peas

3 tbsp kecap manis (sweet soy
sauce)

1 tbsp tomato ketchup

1 to 2 tsp sambal ulek (page 42)

cucumber slices

Preparation time: 45 minutes

1,600 kJ/380 calories per portion

1 Wash the rice until the water runs clear. Place the rice, 40 cl water and a little salt in a heavy saucepan with a tight-fitting lid. Bring the water to the boil, then reduce the heat to very low, and continue to cook the rice, covered, for 15 to 20 minutes. When all the water has been absorbed and the surface of the rice is dry, remove the pan from the heat. Keeping the lid on the pan, leave the rice to stand for about 10 minutes.

2 Meanwhile, rinse the meat under cold, running water, pat dry, then cut across the grain into thin strips. Peel and finely chop the shallots and garlic. Crush the *terasi* with the back of a spoon. Trim and wash the Chinese cabbage and cut into strips about 1 cm wide. Peel the carrot and cut into matchsticks about 5 cm long. Rinse the bean sprouts and shrimps or prawns separately in a colander under cold, running water, then drain thoroughly.

3 Heat the oil in a wok or large frying pan over high heat. Add the meat to the pan a little at a time and stir-fry for about 2 minutes. Add the shrimps and continue to stir-fry for 1 minute more. Remove from the pan and set aside.

4 Add the shallots and garlic to the pan and fry until transparent. Stir in the fresh peas, if using, and cook for about 5 minutes, Add the carrot and stir-fry for about 2 minutes. Add the Chinese cabbage, bean sprouts and the thawed frozen peas, if using, and stir-fry for a further 2 minutes. Finally, return the meat and shrimps or prawns to the pan, add the rice and stir-fry until rice is hot. Season with the *terasi, kecap manis*, tomato ketchup, *sambal ulek* and salt. Mix thoroughly and continue to stir-fry for 2 to 3 minutes.

5 Serve garnished with the cucumber slices—and, if you like, shredded omelette (*see right*)—accompanied by crispy fried onion rings (*page 28*) and prawn crackers (*page 115*).

Shredded omelette
Whisk 2 eggs thoroughly. Fry in a greased frying pan. Leave to cool, then cut into thin shreds.

Note: For best results, use rice cooked the previous day, so that it is nice and dry. This dish is a good way to use up leftover poultry or meat. An alternative way to serve the rice is by packing each portion tightly into a Chinese rice bowl, then turning it out on a plate.

Variation:
Fried noodles (*Bahmi goreng*)
Instead of rice, use 250 g Chinese egg noodles. Cook the noodles in boiling water until *al dente*. Drain, rinse under cold running water, then proceed according to the above recipe.

Fried rice

Fairly easy • National dish

Nasi goreng

Serves 4

200 g long-grain rice
salt
4 shallots
2 garlic cloves
¼ tsp terasi (see page 96)
5 tbsp coconut or vegetable oil
3 tbsp kecap manis (sweet soy sauce)
1 tbsp tomato ketchup
1 to 2 tsp sambal ulek (page 42)
4 eggs
1 sprig fresh coriander (optional)
cucumber slices (optional)

Preparation time: 45 minutes

1,600 kJ/380 calories per portion

1 Wash the rice until the water runs clear. Place the rice, 40 cl water and a little salt in a heavy saucepan with a tight-fitting lid. Bring the water to the boil, then reduce the heat to very low, and continue to cook the rice, covered, for 15 to 20 minutes. When all the water has been absorbed and the surface of the rice is dry, remove the pan from the heat. Keeping the lid on the pan, leave the rice to stand for about 10 minutes.

2 Meanwhile, peel and finely chop the shallots and garlic. Crush the *terasi* with the back of a spoon.

3 When the rice is ready, heat 4 tbsp of the oil in a wok or large frying pan over medium heat and fry the shallots, garlic and *terasi* until transparent. Add the rice and stir-fry for about 3 minutes. Add the *kecap manis*, tomato ketchup and *sambal ulek*, and continue to stir-fry the rice for a further 3 minutes.

4 Heat the remaining oil in a frying pan over medium heat and fry the eggs. Season with a little salt.

5 Arrange the fried rice on four plates and top each portion with a fried egg. Garnish, if you like, with fresh coriander leaves and cucumber slices. Serve accompanied by crispy fried onion rings (*page 28*) and prawn crackers (*page 115*).

Kecap manis

The Southeast Asian-Chinese word, *kecap* or *ketjap*, was brought back by the British from Malaysia. Europeans then adopted a derivation of the word to describe various bottled piquant sauces and, in particular, the tomato sauce known the world over as tomato ketchup (or catsup). However, the Indonesian *kecap* is not tomato sauce at all, but an Indonesian condiment made from fermented soy beans. It is a basic ingredient in nearly all Indonesian sauces and marinades.

The Indonesians use two types of soy sauce, *kecap manis* and *kecap asin*. *Kecap manis* is thick, dark and sweet; it is an essential ingredient of Indonesian cuisine, adding to many dishes both a brown colour and a distinctive, slightly sweet flavour. This sweet soy sauce, which keeps almost indefinitely, should be added only towards the end of cooking, because it burns easily.

Kecap asin is a salty soy sauce, similar to Chinese and Japanese soy sauces, either of which can be used as a substitute if it is unavailable.

Stuffed rice rolls

Lemper ketan

Takes a little time • Spicy

250 g glutinous rice
40 cl canned unsweetened coconut milk
500 g chicken breast fillet
½ bunch thin young spring onions, or 2 to 3 larger ones
3 to 4 garlic cloves
4 shelled kemiri or macadamia nuts
¼ tsp terasi (see page 96)
2 to 3 tbsp coconut oil
½ to 1 tsp sambal ulek (page 42)
½ tsp turmeric
2 tsp ground coriander
1 tsp palm sugar (or, if unavailable, soft brown sugar)
salt
freshly ground black pepper
1 large banana leaf
vegetable oil
10 wooden toothpicks

Preparation time: 1 hour

330 kJ/79 calories per roll

1 Wash the rice until the water runs clear, then drain. Take 30 cl of the coconut milk and pour it with the rice and 40 cl water into a heavy saucepan with a tight-fitting lid. Bring to the boil, then reduce the heat to low and cook the rice, covered, for 15 to 20 minutes. When all the liquid has been absorbed and the surface of the rice is dry, remove the pan from the heat. Keeping the lid on the pan, leave the rice to stand for about 10 minutes.

2 Meanwhile, rinse the chicken breast under cold running water, pat dry and cut across the grain into very thin strips. Trim and wash the spring onions, then cut diagonally into thin rings. Peel and crush the garlic. Finely grate the nuts. Crush the *terasi* with the back of a spoon.

3 Heat the oil in a wok or frying pan over medium heat. Fry the spring onions and garlic for 1 to 2 minutes, until transparent. Increase the heat to high, add the chicken to the pan a little at a time and stir-fry for about 2 minutes. Add the macadamia nuts, *terasi*, *sambal ulek*, turmeric, coriander and palm sugar. Pour in the rest of the coconut milk and continue to cook until the sauce begins to thicken. Season with salt and pepper, and leave to cool a little.

4 Meanwhile, wipe the banana leaf clean with a damp cloth and cut it into 20 rectangles, each about 10 by 15 cm. Brush the inner surface of each piece with a little vegetable oil. Cut the toothpicks in half.

5 Put 1 tbsp of the cooked rice and 1 tsp of the meat mixture on each banana leaf rectangle. Neatly roll up each rectangle, securing the open end with half a toothpick. Serve cold or steam over boiling water in a bamboo or metal steamer, accompanied by a small bowl of additional *sambal ulek*. For a decorative presentation as illustrated opposite, make a diagonal incision in the middle of each roll.

Note: The rolls can be prepared a day in advance. Instead of steaming them, they can also be heated under a grill. The banana leaves are only a wrapping and should not be eaten.

Rice in banana leaves

Fairly easy • Java **Lontong** **Makes 20 rice parcels**

500 g glutinous rice
1 large banana leaf
vegetable oil
20 wooden toothpicks
salt
about 1 tbsp kecap manis
(sweet soy sauce • optional)

Preparation time: 1½ hours
(plus cooling time)

360 kJ/86 calories per parcel

1 Wash the rice until the water runs clear, then drain.

2 Wipe the banana leaf clean with a damp cloth and cut it into 20 squares, each about 15 by 15 cm. Lightly brush the inner side of each square with a little vegetable oil. Cut the wooden toothpicks in half. Roll each square into a cylinder, so that one end overlaps the other by about 2 cm. Secure the lower end of each cylinder with half a toothpick. Spoon about 1 tbsp of the rice into each roll so that it is one third full, leaving the rice room to expand. Secure the top with half a toothpick.

3 Meanwhile, fill a large saucepan half full of water and bring to the boil. Add salt, then place the banana leaf parcels in the boiling water making sure that

they are completely covered. When the water has returned to the boil, reduce the heat to low, cover the pan and cook for about 1 hour, until the rice expands to fill the banana leaf wrappings.

4 Remove the rice parcels from the water with a slotted spoon and leave to cool. The rice will stick together in compact blocks. You can either make a diagonal incision in the middle of each roll and scoop out the rice, or leave the rolls whole. Serve with meat dishes, soups or salads. If you like, season with a little *kecap manis* at the table.

Note: Banana leaves are not edible, but give a delicate flavour to other ingredients. If banana leaves are not available, squares of aluminium foil can be substituted.

Rice with crispy chicken

Fairly easy • Lesser Sunda Islands **Nasi kebuli**

Serves 4

1 oven-ready chicken (about 1.5 kg)
1 bunch thin young spring onions, or
4 to 5 larger ones
3 garlic cloves
4 cm piece fresh ginger or galangal
1 stalk fresh lemon grass
3 cloves
½ to 1 tsp sambal ulek (page 42)
½ tsp turmeric
2 tsp ground coriander
½ tsp cinnamon
salt
200 g long-grain rice
3 to 4 tbsp coconut or vegetable oil

Preparation time: 1¼ hours

3,100 kJ/740 calories per portion

1 Divide the chicken into 8 pieces (*see Note, below*), wash thoroughly and pat dry. Remove most of the skin.

2 Trim and wash the spring onions, then cut them diagonally into thin rings. Peel and crush the garlic. Peel and finely grate the ginger or galangal. Chop the thick lower end of the lemon grass into small pieces. Crush the cloves with a pestle and mortar.

3 Place the chicken in a large pan with a tight-fitting lid together with all the vegetables, spices and salt, cover with ½ litre water and bring to the boil. Reduce the heat to medium and cook, covered, for about 20 minutes.

4 Wash the rice until the water runs clear, then drain. When the chicken is cooked, remove it from the stock and sprinkle in the rice. Replace the lid and cook over low heat for about 20 minutes, until all the stock is absorbed and the surface of the rice is dry.

5 Heat the oil in a wok or large frying pan. Fry the chicken, in batches if necessary, until crisp all over. Arrange the rice and chicken pieces on a serving dish or, as below, in a decorative leaf-covered basket tray.

Note: To divide a chicken evenly into 8 pieces, remove the neck from the body with poultry shears. Cut the breast in half along the breast bone. Turn the chicken over, and cut the back in half with a meat cleaver. Separate the wings at the upper joint. Remove any bone splinters from the chicken pieces.

SAMBALS AND CURRIES

The Indonesians are very fond of turning meat, fish or vegetables into sambals or curries. Their searingly hot sambals use what might seem to Westerners an excessive amount of spices, dominated by red or green chili peppers—*sambal* is the Indonesian word for chili sauce. Sambals range from simple condiments made from crushed chili peppers, such as *sambal oelek*, to fried vegetable, egg, meat, fish or seafood dishes.

The term "curry" comes from the Indian word *kari*, and was used in Britain in the early 19th century to describe a mixture of spices sold commercially as curry powder. In India, the land where curries originated, it meant a very specific method of preparing vegetables, meat, fish or seafood. First introduced to Indonesia by Indian traders, this style of cookery soon became popular, especially in Sumatra.

Many Indian curries include yogurt, but, in Indonesia, coconut milk has replaced the yogurt, which is practically unknown there. So Indonesian curries have their own distinctive, mild flavour.

Take care when handling chilies, because their volatile oils can irritate the skin and cause eyes to burn if you rub them. Wash your hands, knife and chopping board immediately after use. If you have sensitive skin, it is a good idea to wear disposable gloves.

Chili sauce
Sambal ulek

Makes 10 tsp

**10 fresh red chili peppers
(see Glossary)
4 tbsp sunflower oil
salt**

Preparation time: 15 minutes

120 kJ/29 calories per tsp

1 Wash the chili peppers and chop into thick rings, retaining the seeds, but discarding the stalks. Put the chilies in a mortar with the sunflower oil and some salt, and crush with a pestle. For a smoother sauce, you can purée the mixture in a blender.

2 Heat the chili mixture in a small frying pan, stirring constantly, for about 10 minutes, until the oil rises to the surface. Allow to cool.

3 Serve *sambal ulek* with rice dishes, and as a condiment to add spice to meat, fish and vegetable dishes.

Variation:
Spicy chili sauce (*Sambal bajak*)
To the mixture of chili peppers, oil and salt, add 4 to 5 finely sliced spring onions, 5 chopped garlic cloves, 5 finely grated macadamia nuts, and ¼ tsp crushed *terasi*. Heat the paste for about 2 minutes in a frying pan, stirring constantly. Add 15 cl coconut milk. Simmer over low heat for about 10 minutes, stirring from time to time.

Note: You can buy jars of ready-made *sambal ulek* in any well-stocked supermarket or Asian food shop. Home-made *sambal ulek* will keep in the refrigerator for about 2 weeks.

Chili-soy sauce
Sambal kecap

Makes 1 jar

**1 to 2 fresh red chili peppers (see
Glossary)
3 garlic cloves
¼ bunch thin young spring onions,
or 1 to 2 larger ones
20 cl soy sauce**

Preparation time: 15 minutes

720 kJ/170 calories per jar

1 Wash the chili peppers. Cut them in half lengthwise, discarding the seeds and stalks. Cut the halves into thin strips. Peel and crush the garlic. Trim and wash the spring onions, and cut them into thin rings.

2 Place the chilies, crushed garlic and spring onion rings in a small bowl. Add the soy sauce and stir all the ingredients together. This sambal goes well with any rice dish.

Variation:
Sweet chili-soy sauce
(*Sambal kecap manis*)
Substitute sweet soy sauce (*kecap manis*) for the salty soy sauce.

Note: Spring onions are a good source of Vitamin C and also contain vitamins B_1, B_2 and B_6. Indonesian spring onions grow in clumps; they are more slender than their European equivalents, with a milder aromatic flavour.

Chili-tomato sauce

Quick and easy • Very hot   **Sambal cobek**   *Serves 4*

2 large beef tomatoes
2 garlic cloves
2 fresh red or green chili peppers
(see Glossary)
pinch of terasi (see page 96)
salt
1 red chili flower (Note, page 112)

Preparation time: 15 minutes

58 kJ/14 calories per portion

1 Plunge the tomatoes into boiling water, skin them and finely chop the flesh. Peel and crush the garlic. Wash the 2 chili peppers, cut them in half lengthwise, remove seeds and stalks, then cut into thin strips. Crush the *terasi* with the back of a spoon.

2 Put all the ingredients, including the *terasi*, in a small bowl and stir thoroughly. If you prefer a smoother sauce, blend them in a food processor. Serve with any rice dish, garnished with the chili flower.

Note: This sambal takes its name from the *cobek*, the wooden mortar in which Indonesians grind chili peppers.

The fieriness of chili peppers can be toned down by coconut milk or cucumber. If you have eaten something that really is too hot for your taste, eat a tablespoonful or two of grated coconut, fresh or dried. Yogurt or hot tea also provide relief. Water or other cold drinks are not suitable.

Eggs in chili sauce

Telur belado

Not difficult • Lesser Sunda Islands

Serves 4

8 eggs
2 to 3 fresh red or green chili peppers (see Glossary)
½ bunch thin young spring onions, or 2 to 3 larger ones
3 garlic cloves
4 cm piece fresh ginger
1 stalk fresh lemon grass
¼ tsp terasi (see page 96)
2 tbsp coconut oil
¼ litre canned unsweetened coconut milk
2 tsp palm sugar (or, if unavailable, soft brown sugar)
salt

Preparation time: 25 minutes

640 kJ/150 calories per portion

1 Place the eggs in a saucepan with enough water to cover, and boil over medium heat for 8 to 10 minutes. Remove from the water, plunge into cold water, then shell carefully.

2 While the eggs are boiling, prepare the rest of the ingredients. Wash the chili peppers, cut them in half lengthwise and remove the seeds and stalks. Cut the halves into thin strips. Trim and wash the spring onions and cut them into thin rings. Peel and crush the garlic. Peel and finely grate the ginger. Wash the lemon grass and finely chop the thick, lower part. Crush the *terasi* with the back of a spoon.

3 Heat the oil in a wok or deep frying pan over medium heat. Stir-fry the chili peppers, spring onions, garlic, ginger, lemon grass and *terasi* for 2 to 3 minutes. Stir in the coconut milk and the palm sugar and allow the sauce to thicken slightly.

4 Place the eggs—either whole or cut in half—in the sauce. Reduce the heat to low, cover the pan and simmer for about 3 minutes. Season with salt. Serve with rice and, if you like, cucumber salad and prawn crackers (*page 115*).

Chicken liver sambal

Fairly easy • Sulawesi

Sambal goreng hati

Serves 4

1 walnut-sized piece compressed tamarind pulp
500 g chicken livers
250 g bean sprouts
3 fresh red or green chili peppers (see Glossary)
4 shallots
1 stalk fresh lemon grass
¼ tsp terasi (see page 96)
2 to 3 tbsp coconut oil
2 tsp palm sugar (or, if unavailable, soft brown sugar)
¼ litre canned unsweetened coconut milk
salt • 3 sprigs fresh coriander

Preparation time: 45 minutes

2,100 kJ/500 calories per portion

1 Put the tamarind pulp in a bowl with 10 cl hot water and leave to soak for about 10 minutes, then knead thoroughly to produce a thick juice. Discard any hard bits or seeds and strain through a sieve.

2 While the tamarind is soaking, wash the chicken livers thoroughly, pat dry and shred finely. Plunge the bean sprouts into hot water, then drain.

3 Wash the chili peppers, cut in half lengthwise and remove the seeds and stalks. Cut the halves diagonally into thin strips. Peel, halve and thinly slice the shallots. Wash the lemon grass and finely chop the thick, lower end. Crush the *terasi* with the back of a spoon.

4 Heat the oil in a frying pan over high heat. Fry the chicken livers in batches for about 2 minutes until browned all over. Remove them from the pan and keep warm.

5 Add the chili peppers, shallots and lemon grass to the pan and fry for 2 to 3 minutes, until transparent. Add the bean sprouts and continue to stir-fry for about 1 minute. Stir in the *terasi* and sugar, then the tamarind juice. Add the coconut milk and bring to the boil. Immediately reduce the heat to low and stir in the reserved chicken livers. Simmer for 1 to 2 minutes. Season with salt and garnish with coriander leaves. Serve with rice.

Beef sambal

Fairly easy • Lesser Sunda Islands

Sambal goreng daging

Serves 4

750 g fillet or rump steak
4 tomatoes
3 to 4 red chili peppers (see Glossary)
1 bunch thin young spring onions, or 4 to 5 larger ones
3 to 4 garlic cloves
4 cm piece fresh ginger
1 stalk fresh lemon grass
¼ tsp terasi (see page 96)
3 to 4 tbsp coconut or vegetable oil
2 tsp ground coriander
1 tsp palm sugar (or, if unavailable, soft brown sugar)
salt

Preparation time: 1 hour
1,300 kJ/310 calories per portion

1 Rinse the meat under cold running water, pat dry and cut into cubes. Plunge the tomatoes briefly into boiling water and skin them. Cut in half, remove the seeds and finely chop the flesh. Wash the chili peppers, cut in half lengthwise, remove the seeds and cut into thin strips. Trim and wash the spring onions, then cut them diagonally into 3 cm-long pieces. Peel and crush the garlic. Peel and finely grate the ginger. Wash the lemon grass and finely chop the thick, lower end. Crush the *terasi* with the back of a spoon.

2 Heat the oil in a wok or heavy saucepan over high heat. Add the meat in batches and stir-fry, until brown all over. Remove the meat from the pan and keep warm. Add the chili peppers, spring onions, garlic, ginger, lemon grass and *terasi* to the pan and stir-fry for 3 to 5 minutes, until transparent. Stir in the coriander, palm sugar and chopped tomatoes. Stir in the meat, cover the pan and cook over a low heat for 5 to 10 minutes, until the meat is tender. Season with salt. Serve with rice and *sambal ulek* (*page 42*).

Variation:
Fried lamb (*Sambal goreng kambing*) Substitute lamb fillet for the beef in the above recipe.

Fried squid sambal

A little more complex • Sulawesi **Sambal goreng cumi cumi** *Serves 4*

1 walnut-sized piece compressed tamarind pulp
600 g small fresh or frozen squid or cuttlefish, cleaned and ready to cook
3 to 4 fresh chili peppers (see Glossary)
1 bunch thin young spring onions, or 4 to 5 larger ones
5 garlic cloves
4 cm piece fresh ginger
2 tsp palm sugar
2 to 3 tbsp coconut or vegetable oil
salt

Preparation time: 45 minutes

700 kJ/170 calories per portion

1 Soak the tamarind pulp in 20 cl hot water and follow instructions on page 46, Step 1, top recipe.

2 While the tamarind is soaking, rinse the squid or cuttlefish thoroughly under cold running water and pat dry. Cut the body pouches into bite-sized rings and separate the tentacles.

3 Wash the chili peppers, cut them in half lengthwise and remove the seeds and stalks. Cut the halves diagonally into thin strips. Trim and wash the spring onions, and cut them diagonally into thin rings. Reserve a few green rings for garnish. Peel and crush the garlic. Peel and finely grate the ginger.

4 Put all the prepared ingredients, except the tamarind juice and reserved spring onion rings, in a bowl. Add the sugar and stir to form a thick paste.

5 Heat the oil in a wok or large frying pan over high heat. Fry the squid in batches for about 5 minutes, until browned all over. Add the spicy paste and stir-fry for a further 3 minutes. Pour in the tamarind juice and season with salt. Reduce the heat to medium, cover the pan and cook for 15 to 20 minutes. Garnish with the reserved spring onion rings. Serve with rice.

Squid, cuttlefish and octopus

Squid and cuttlefish, the most common of the edible cephalopods—molluscs with sucker-bearing tentacles—are found in oceans throughout the world. The eight-armed octopus, caught in the tropical waters of Indonesia as well as the Mediterranean, is especially prized in the kitchen.

Freshly caught seafood of all kinds is to be found in the islands' fish markets. The tender meat of the body sac and tentacles of baby octopus and squid are delicious fried. Larger specimens, however, benefit from being tenderized with a hammer and need longer to cook. Cuttlefish and squid are also delicious stuffed and braised.

To clean, the cuttlebone of the cuttlefish and the quill-like pen of the squid are removed, together with the viscera, ink sac, beak and the body sac's translucent skin. The sac should be rinsed inside and out under running water,

Fried prawn sambal

Sambal goreng udang

Fairly easy • Java   *Serves 4*

2 to 3 fresh red or green chili peppers (see Glossary)
3 garlic cloves
4 cm piece fresh ginger
1 stalk fresh lemon grass
¼ bunch thin young spring onions, or 1 to 2 larger ones
2 tsp palm sugar (or, if unavailable, soft brown sugar)
500 g peeled, cooked king prawns
2 to 3 tbsp coconut oil
¼ litre canned unsweetened coconut milk
salt

Preparation time: 30 minutes

1,900 kJ/450 calories per portion

1 Wash the chili peppers, cut them in half lengthwise and discard the seeds and stalks. Cut the halves into thin strips. Peel and crush the garlic. Peel and finely grate the ginger. Wash the lemon grass and finely chop the thicker end. Trim and wash the spring onions, and cut them into pieces about 5 cm long, then into fine strips. Set aside a few strips of spring onion for garnish.

2 Put the chili peppers, garlic, ginger, lemon grass and the sugar in a bowl and stir together to form a thick paste. Rinse the prawns in a colander under cold running water and pat dry.

3 Heat the oil in a wok over medium heat. Fry the paste until transparent. Add the spring onions and stir-fry for about 1 minute. Add the prawns and stir-fry very briefly. Pour in the coconut milk, reduce the heat to low and simmer for about 3 minutes until cooked through. Season with salt and sprinkle with the reserved spring onion strips. Serve with rice and prawn crackers (*page 115*).

Variation: Sweet-and-sour prawn sambal (*Udang goreng asam manis*) Instead of coconut milk, use ¼ litre tamarind juice, made from 1 walnut-sized piece compressed tamarind pulp soaked in hot water (*see below*).

Aubergine sambal

Sambal goreng terong

Fairly easy • Lesser Sunda Islands   *Serves 4*

1 walnut-sized piece compressed tamarind pulp
2 fresh red chili peppers (see Glossary)
1 bunch thin young spring onions, or 4 to 5 larger ones
4 to 5 garlic cloves
¼ tsp terasi (see page 96)
2 large aubergines
6 tbsp coconut or vegetable oil
3 tsp palm sugar (or, if unavailable, soft brown sugar)
1½ tsp ground coriander
salt
3 sprigs fresh coriander

Preparation time: 50 minutes

730 kJ/170 calories per portion

1 Put the tamarind pulp in a bowl with ¼ litre hot water to soak, and follow instructions on page 46, Step 1, top recipe.

2 While the tamarind is soaking, wash the chili peppers, cut them in half lengthwise and discard the seeds and stalks. Cut the halves diagonally into thin strips. Trim and wash the spring onions. Cut the green parts into 5 cm-long pieces, then into thin strips, and set aside. Cut the rest into thin rings. Peel and finely chop the garlic. Crush the *terasi* with the back of a spoon.

3 Remove the stalks and wash the aubergines. Cut them lengthwise into 1 cm-thick slices, then dice.

4 Heat the oil in a fireproof casserole or heavy saucepan over medium heat. Fry the chili peppers, spring onion rings and garlic until transparent. Add the diced aubergines and fry until browned all over. Stir in the *terasi* and sugar, then the tamarind juice. Season with coriander and salt, and continue to cook for 20 to 25 minutes. Serve garnished with coriander leaves and the reserved strips of spring onion.

Cauliflower with chilies

Tumis kembang kol

Not difficult • Java

Serves 4

1 cauliflower (about 1 kg)
3 fresh red chili peppers (see Glossary)
½ bunch thin young spring onions, or 2 to 3 larger ones
3 garlic cloves
4 cm piece fresh ginger
¼ tsp terasi (see page 96)
3 to 4 tbsp coconut or vegetable oil
1 tbsp soy sauce
2 tbsp kecap manis (sweet soy sauce)

Preparation time: 40 minutes

540 kJ/130 calories per portion

1 Remove the stalks and leaves from the cauliflower, wash and divide into bite-sized florets. Wash the chili peppers, cut them in half lengthwise and discard the seeds and stalks. Cut lengthwise into thin strips. Trim and wash the spring onions, and cut them diagonally into thin rings. Peel and crush the garlic. Peel and finely grate the ginger. Crush the *terasi* with the back of a spoon.

2 Bring some salted water to the boil in a saucepan and add the cauliflower. When the water returns to the boil, reduce the heat to medium, cover the pan, and cook the cauliflower for about 10 minutes until tender but still crisp.

3 Meanwhile, heat the oil in a wok or fireproof casserole over medium heat. Stir-fry the chili peppers, spring onions, garlic and ginger for about 3 minutes, until transparent. Add the *terasi*. Pour in the soy sauce, *kecap manis* and 10 cl water, and stir until the sauce thickens slightly.

4 Strain the cauliflower through a large colander and add it to the pan. Stir, then reduce the heat to low and simmer for a further 3 minutes. Serve with rice and *sambal ulek* (*page 42*).

Note: When frying chili peppers, switch on your kitchen extractor fan, as steam from chilies can be unpleasant.

Green bean sambal

Sambal goreng buncis

Not difficult • Java

Serves 4

750 g green beans • salt
3 fresh red chili peppers (see Glossary)
½ bunch thin young spring onions, or 2 to 3 larger ones
3 garlic cloves
4 cm piece fresh ginger
¼ tsp terasi (see page 96)
3 to 4 tbsp coconut oil
3 tsp palm sugar (or, if unavailable, soft brown sugar)
20 cl canned unsweetened coconut milk

Preparation time: 40 minutes

1,600 kJ/380 calories per portion

1 Wash and trim the beans. Bring a pan of lightly salted water to the boil. Add the beans and boil for about 5 minutes, then strain.

2 Wash the chili peppers, cut them in half lengthwise and discard the seeds and stalks. Cut lengthwise into thin strips. Trim and wash the spring onions and cut them into thin rings. Peel and crush the garlic. Peel and finely grate the ginger. Crush the *terasi* with the back of a spoon.

3 Heat the oil in a wok or fireproof casserole over medium heat. Stir-fry the chili peppers, spring onions, garlic and ginger for about 3 minutes, until transparent. Add the *terasi* and sugar. Pour in the coconut milk and let the sauce thicken slightly. Stir in the beans, reduce the heat to low and cook for a further 5 minutes. Season with salt. Serve with rice and prawn crackers (*page 115*).

Note: This recipe and the aubergine sambal on page 51 are examples of the diversity of vegetables and other ingredients used in Indonesian sambals. Much imagination goes into creating them; they can be crisp, fiery or spicy. Try making them with Chinese cabbage, broccoli, courgettes or tofu.

Jackfruit curry

Gulai nangka

500 g beef (sirloin or rump)
5 shallots
2 garlic cloves
4 cm piece fresh ginger
4 shelled macadamia nuts
1 tsp sambal ulek (page 42)
½ tsp ground turmeric
1 tsp ground coriander
salt
1 can jackfruit (about 325 g drained) or bamboo shoots
3 sprigs fresh coriander
2 to 3 tbsp coconut oil
40 cl canned unsweetened coconut milk
3 curry leaves or bay leaves

Preparation time: 1½ hours

2,900 kJ/690 calories per portion

1 Rinse the beef under cold running water, pat dry with kitchen paper, then cut across the grain into thin slices.

2 Peel and finely chop the shallots and garlic. Peel and finely grate the ginger. Finely grate the macadamia nuts. Mix the shallots, garlic and ginger with the *sambal ulek*, turmeric, ground coriander and a little salt, and work into a paste. Place the jackfruit or bamboo shoots in a colander, rinse under cold running water, drain, and cut into 2 cm pieces. Wash the fresh coriander, pat dry and chop finely.

3 Heat the oil in a wok or fireproof casserole. Fry the spicy paste for about 3 minutes until transparent. Add the meat in batches and fry over high heat for about 10 minutes until browned all over. Add the coconut milk and stir to incorporate the pan juices. Add the curry leaves or bay leaves and bring to the boil. Reduce the heat to low, cover, and cook for about 1 hour. About 10 minutes before the end of cooking, add the jackfruit or bamboo shoots.

3 Discard the curry or bay leaves and season with salt. Transfer to a serving dish, sprinkle with the chopped coriander and serve with rice and cucumber slices.

Note: Jackfruit, a large fruit related to the breadfruit, is eaten raw when ripe or picked before ripening and cooked like a vegetable. It gives this mild curry an unusual sweetish flavour.

Spiced beef in coconut milk

Rendang

Fairly easy • Western Sumatra

Serves 4

1 walnut-sized piece compressed
tamarind pulp
1 kg boned shoulder of beef
5 shallots • 5 garlic cloves
4 cm piece fresh ginger
1 to 2 spring onions
4 to 5 tbsp coconut oil
1 to 2 tsp sambal ulek (page 42)
½ tsp turmeric
2 tsp ground coriander
1 tsp ground cumin
½ tsp freshly ground black pepper
2 tsp palm sugar (or, if unavailable,
soft brown sugar)
40 cl canned unsweetened
coconut milk
salt • fresh coriander
crispy fried onion rings (page 28)

Preparation time: 1½ to 2 hours

1,800 kJ/430 calories per portion

1 Soak the tamarind pulp in 20 cl hot water and follow instructions on page 46, Step 1, top recipe.

2 While the tamarind is soaking, rinse the beef under cold running water, pat dry with kitchen paper and cut into 2 cm cubes. Peel and finely chop the shallots and garlic. Peel and finely grate the ginger. Trim and wash the spring onion and cut into rings.

3 Heat the oil in a wok or fireproof casserole. Fry the shallots, garlic and ginger until lightly browned. Add the meat in batches and stir-fry over high heat until browned. Stir in the *sambal ulek*, turmeric, ground coriander, cumin, pepper and sugar, and stir-fry for about 3 minutes.

4 Stir in the tamarind juice, followed by the coconut milk. Bring the sauce to the boil, then simmer for 7 to 8 minutes, stirring constantly, until the fat rises to the surface. Season with salt. Cover the pan and simmer the curry over low heat for 1 to 1½ hours. Garnish with the spring onion rings, coriander leaves and crispy fried onion rings. Serve warm or cold with rice, prawn crackers (*page 115*) and additional *sambal ulek*.

Variation:

Lamb curry *(Gulai kambing)*
Use lean lamb instead of beef, adding 1 to 2 grated blades of mace. Replace the ginger with galangal. According to the size of the pieces of meat, reduce the cooking time by ½ hour, if necessary.

Calf's liver curry

Gulai hati

Fairly easy • Western Sumatra

Serves 4

750 g calf's liver
6 shallots
3 garlic cloves
4 cm piece fresh ginger
1 stalk fresh lemon grass
10 shelled kemiri or macadamia nuts
1 to 2 tsp sambal ulek (page 42)
½ tsp turmeric
1 tsp ground coriander
3 to 4 tbsp coconut oil
40 cl canned unsweetened coconut milk
salt

Preparation time: 40 minutes

1,500 kJ/360 calories per portion

1 Carefully skin the liver, rinse under cold running water, pat dry and cut into bite-sized pieces. Peel and finely chop the shallots and garlic. Peel and finely grate the ginger. Trim and wash the lemon grass and finely chop the thick, lower end. Finely grate the nuts. Put the shallots, garlic, ginger, lemon grass and nuts in a bowl with the *sambal ulek*, turmeric and coriander and stir to form a thick paste.

2 Heat the oil in a wok over high heat. Add the liver to the pan in batches and brown for 2 to 3 minutes. Remove from the pan and keep warm. Add the spicy paste and stir-fry for 3 to 5 minutes. Pour in the coconut milk, then cook the sauce for a further 5 minutes, stirring

constantly, until it thickens. Return the liver to the pan, reduce the heat to low, cover, and simmer for 2 to 3 minutes. Season with salt and serve with rice garnished, if you like, with strips of red chili pepper, prawn crackers (*page 115*) and chili-soy sauce (*page 42*).

Variation:

Lamb's liver curry (*Hati goreng Bali*) Make a paste from 3 chopped garlic cloves, 3 chopped shallots, 1 tsp turmeric, ½ tsp *sambal ulek* and 1 tsp peanut oil. Cut 500 g lamb's liver into bite-sized pieces, and coat in the paste. Brown the liver in 2 tbsp oil and moisten with ¼ litre coconut milk. Cook until the sauce thickens and season with the juice of ½ lemon, salt and pepper.

Chicken curry

Kari ayam

Fairly easy • Western Sumatra

Serves 4

1 oven-ready chicken (about 1.5 kg)
6 shallots • 3 garlic cloves
4 cm piece fresh ginger
1 stalk fresh lemon grass
¼ tsp terasi (see page 96)
5 shelled kemiri or macadamia nuts
1 tsp sambal ulek (page 42)
½ tsp turmeric
1 tsp ground coriander
½ tsp freshly ground black pepper
salt • 4 to 5 tbsp coconut oil
40 cl canned unsweetened coconut milk
2 curry leaves or bay leaves

Preparation time: 1 hour

4,500 kJ/1,100 calories per portion

1 Divide the chicken into 8 pieces (*see Note, page 39*), wash thoroughly and pat dry, discarding all bone splinters. Remove most of the skin.

2 Peel and finely dice the shallots and garlic. Peel and finely grate the ginger. Trim and wash the lemon grass and finely chop the thick, lower end. Crush the *terasi* with the back of a spoon. Finely grate the nuts. Put the shallots, garlic, ginger, lemon grass, *terasi* and nuts in a bowl with the *sambal ulek*, turmeric, coriander, pepper and a little salt, and stir them together to form a thick paste.

3 Heat the oil in a wok or fireproof casserole over medium heat. Add the spicy paste and stir-fry for about 3 minutes. Add the chicken pieces in batches and fry until well browned. Stir in the coconut milk. Add the curry or bay leaves, reduce the heat to low and cook, covered, for 20 to 30 minutes, turning the chicken pieces from time to time. Discard the curry or bay leaves. Serve, garnished, if you like, with shredded chili pepper, accompanied by rice, cucumber slices, prawn crackers (*page 115*) and *sambal ulek* (*page 42*).

Note: The rest of the lemon grass can be chopped and brewed with tea.

Curried noodles

Mie kuah

A little more complex • Sumatra

Serves 4

2 stalks fresh lemon grass
3 garlic cloves
4 cm piece fresh ginger
1 bunch thin young spring onions,
or 4 to 5 larger ones
1 tsp sambal ulek (page 42)
½ tsp turmeric
2 tsp ground coriander
salt
250 g boned chicken breasts
2 to 3 tbsp coconut oil
40 cl canned unsweetened
coconut milk
250 g bean sprouts
250 g Chinese egg noodles
2 to 3 tbsp kecap manis (sweet soy
sauce)

Preparation time: 45 minutes

1,600 kJ/380 calories per portion

1 Trim and wash the lemon grass and finely chop the thick, lower end (*above*). Peel and crush the garlic.

2 Peel the ginger and cut it into thin slices (*above*), then dice the slices. Trim and wash the spring onions, and cut into thin rings. Put the lemon grass, garlic, ginger and spring onion in a bowl with the *sambal ulek*, turmeric, coriander and salt, and stir to form a thick paste. Rinse the chicken under running water, pat dry and cut into 15 mm cubes.

3 Heat the oil in a wok or fireproof casserole. Add the spicy paste and stir-fry for 2 to 3 minutes. Add the meat to the pan in batches and stir-fry over high heat for 5 to 10 minutes. Reduce the heat, stir in the coconut milk and let the sauce cook until it thickens slightly. Cover the pan, and cook over low heat for a further 3 to 5 minutes.

4 Meanwhile, briefly blanch the bean sprouts in boiling water.

5 Bring a pan of salted water to the boil. Place the noodles in the boiling water. Using two forks, separate the noodle nests (*above*), then cook according to the instructions on the packet until the noodles are *al dente*. Drain and rinse with cold water.

6 Add the bean sprouts to the wok or casserole, stir, then simmer for about 2 minutes. Finally, stir in the cooked noodles and *kecap manis*. Serve warm or cold.

Variation:
Curried noodles with tofu (*Mie tahu*) Prepare the curried noodles as described above, adding 250 g tofu, cut into 1 cm-thick slices, to the sauce at the same time as the bean sprouts. Stir carefully, to avoid the tofu falling apart.

Note: To save time and effort when preparing the spicy paste, purée all the ingredients in a blender, adding a little oil if necessary.

Fish curry

Gulai ikan

Fairly easy • Sumatra

Serves 4

1 walnut-sized piece compressed
tamarind pulp
800 g firm-fleshed fish fillets (cod,
redfish, haddock or pollack)
salt • juice of ½ lemon
4 shallots • 2 garlic cloves
4 cm piece fresh ginger
1 stalk fresh lemon grass
¼ tsp terasi (see page 96)
½ to 1 tsp sambal ulek (page 42)
½ tsp turmeric • 2 tsp ground coriander
3 to 4 tbsp coconut oil
40 cl canned unsweetened
coconut milk
1 sprig fresh coriander

Preparation time: 45 minutes

2,800 kJ/670 calories per portion

1 Soak the tamarind pulp in 15 cl hot water and follow instructions on page 46, Step 1, top recipe.

2 While the tamarind is soaking, rinse the fish fillets under cold running water and pat dry. Remove any skin, then cut into 2 cm cubes. Sprinkle with salt and the lemon juice. Peel and finely chop the shallots and garlic. Peel and finely grate the ginger. Trim and wash the lemon grass and finely chop the thick, lower end. Crush the *terasi* with the back of a spoon.

3 Put the shallots, garlic, ginger, lemon grass and *terasi* in a bowl with the *sambal ulek*, turmeric and ground coriander and stir together to form a thick paste.

4 Heat the oil in a wok or fireproof casserole over high heat. Fry the fish in batches for 2 to 4 minutes, until browned all over. Remove the fish from the pan and keep warm. Reduce the heat to medium, add the spicy paste and stir-fry for 3 to 5 minutes. Pour in the tamarind juice. Reduce the heat to low and add the coconut milk. Simmer the sauce, uncovered, for 2 to 3 minutes. Finally, stir in the fish and simmer for a further 3 minutes. Season with salt and sprinkle with coriander leaves—and, if you like, some red chili pepper rings. Serve with rice.

Curried squid

Gulai cumi cumi

Fairly easy • Sumatra

Serves 4

1 walnut-sized piece compressed
tamarind pulp
600 g small fresh or frozen squid or
cuttlefish, cleaned and ready to cook
3 shallots • 2 garlic cloves
4 cm piece fresh ginger
1 stalk fresh lemon grass
¼ tsp terasi (see page 96)
4 shelled kemiri or macadamia nuts
1 tsp sambal ulek (page 42)
½ tsp turmeric • 2 tsp ground coriander
2 tsp palm sugar • 3 to 4 tbsp coconut
oil
¼ litre unsweetened coconut milk
salt

Preparation time: 45 minutes
2,000 kJ/480 calories per portion

1 Soak the tamarind pulp in 10 cl hot water and follow instructions on page 46, Step 1, top recipe.

2 Meanwhile, rinse the squid or cuttlefish (thawed, if frozen) thoroughly under cold running water, then pat dry. Cut the body pouches in half lengthwise, then into narrow, bite-sized pieces; separate the tentacles.

3 Peel and finely dice the shallots and garlic. Peel and finely grate the ginger. Trim and wash the lemon grass and finely chop the thick, lower end. Crush the *terasi* with the back of a spoon. Finely grate the nuts. Put the shallots, garlic, ginger, lemon grass, *terasi* and nuts in a bowl with the *sambal ulek*, turmeric, coriander and sugar. Stir to form a thick paste.

4 Heat the oil in a wok or fireproof casserole until sizzling. Fry the squid or cuttlefish in batches for about 5 minutes until brown all over. Add the spicy paste and stir-fry for about 3 minutes. Pour in the tamarind juice, followed by the coconut milk. Reduce the heat to low, cover the pan and simmer for 15 to 20 minutes until the squid or cuttlefish is tender. Season with salt. Serve with rice and a bowl of *sambal ulek*.

Mixed vegetable curry

Not difficult • Sumatra   **Kari sayur**   *Serves 4*

5 shallots • 3 garlic cloves
4 cm piece fresh ginger
2 stalks fresh lemon grass
½ tsp terasi (see page 96)
1 tsp sambal ulek (page 42)
½ tsp turmeric • 2 tsp ground cumin
2 tsp ground coriander
1 tsp freshly ground black pepper
salt
2 tsp palm sugar (or, if unavailable,
soft brown sugar)
300 g green beans
300 g floury potatoes
300 g white cabbage
2 to 3 tbsp coconut oil
60 cl canned unsweetened
coconut milk
2 curry leaves or bay leaves
2 red chili flowers (Note, page 112)

Preparation time: 1¼ hours

3,500 kJ/830 calories per portion

1 Peel and finely chop the shallots and garlic. Peel and finely grate the ginger. Trim and wash the lemon grass and finely chop the thick, lower ends. Crush the *terasi* with the back of a spoon. Put the shallots, garlic, ginger, lemon grass and *terasi* in a bowl with the *sambal ulek*, turmeric, cumin, coriander, salt, pepper and sugar. Stir together to form a thick paste.

2 Wash and trim the beans, then cut diagonally into 4 cm pieces. Peel the potatoes and cut them into small cubes. Trim and wash the cabbage, removing the stalks and tough ribs. Cut the leaves into strips about 1 cm wide.

3 Heat the oil in a wok or saucepan. Stir-fry the curry paste over a medium heat for 3 to 5 minutes. Add the beans and continue to fry for a further 5 minutes. Stir in the diced potatoes and shredded cabbage. Pour in the coconut milk, add the curry or bay leaves, then cover the pan and cook over a medium heat for about 30 to 35 minutes, stirring from time to time. Discard the curry or bay leaves and season with salt. Garnish with the chili flowers and serve with rice and *sambal ulek*.

Aubergine curry

Fairly easy • Sumatra **Terong masak santen**   *Serves 4*

**1 walnut-sized piece compressed
tamarind pulp
1 bunch thin young spring onions, or
4 to 5 larger ones
5 garlic cloves • 4 cm piece fresh ginger
1 stalk fresh lemon grass
¼ tsp terasi (see page 96)
1 tsp sambal ulek (page 42)
½ tsp turmeric
2 tsp ground coriander
2 tsp ground cumin • salt
2 tsp palm or soft brown sugar
2 large aubergines
5 to 6 tbsp coconut oil
½ litre unsweetened coconut milk**

Preparation time: 1 hour

3,000 kJ/710 calories per portion

1 Soak the tamarind pulp in 15 cl hot water and follow instructions on page 46, Step 1, top recipe.

2 While the tamarind is soaking, trim and wash the spring onions and cut them into thin rings. Peel and crush the garlic. Peel and finely grate the ginger. Trim and wash the lemon grass and finely chop the thick, lower end. Crush the *terasi* with the back of a spoon. Put the spring onions—setting aside 1 tbsp for garnish—the garlic, ginger, lemon grass and *terasi* in a bowl with the *sambal ulek*, turmeric, coriander, cumin, salt and sugar. Stir everything together to form a thick paste.

3 Trim and wash the aubergines. Cut them lengthwise into slices about 1 cm thick, then into dice.

4 Heat the oil in a wok or fireproof casserole over medium heat. Stir-fry the diced aubergines in batches for about 3 minutes. Add the curry paste and continue to stir-fry briefly. Stir in the tamarind juice, then the coconut milk. Reduce the heat to low and simmer, covered, for 20 to 25 minutes. Season with salt. Serve hot or cold, garnished with the reserved spring onion rings and accompanied by plain rice, a bowl of sweet chili-soy sauce (page 42) and prawn crackers (*page 115*).

MEAT, POULTRY AND FISH

I ndonesia's most famous national
dish is satay: marinated cubes of
beef, lamb or chicken threaded onto
skewers, grilled over charcoal, and
eaten dipped in a sweet and spicy
peanut sauce. Satays are served
everywhere, from the best restaurants
to simple street-corner food stalls.

Except on Bali, the majority of
Indonesians are Muslims and do not
eat pork. Beef, taken mostly from water
buffalo, is expensive and regarded as
a treat for special occasions rather
than everyday fare. As a result, and
because poultry is easy to rear and
comparatively cheap, chicken, and to
a lesser extent duck, is the most
popular meat. But there are many
delicious meat dishes, including pork
specialities from Bali, where there is
a large Hindu population.

In an island nation such as Indonesia,
the sea is an important source of food.
The local markets offer a huge variety
of fish and shellfish, both fresh and—
because they spoil quickly in the hot
climate—dried. Many country-dwellers
supplement their diet with fish farmed
in the flooded paddy fields.

The fish or seafood is prepared in
many different ways. Fish such as sea
bass, sea bream or grey mullet may be

served whole grilled over a charcoal
fire or baked, wrapped in a banana
leaf. Or it may be cut small and deep-
fried in batter or cooked in a highly
seasoned sauce.

Beef or chicken satay

Not difficult • National dish   Saté   *Serves 4*

750 g fillet of beef or chicken
40 wooden skewers about
20 cm long
3 tbsp soy sauce
3 tbsp kecap manis (sweet
soy sauce)
1 tsp sambal ulek (page 42)

For the peanut sauce:
2 shallots • 3 garlic cloves
200 g roasted peanuts
4 tbsp kecap manis
1 tsp sambal ulek • juice of ½ lemon
3 tsp palm or soft brown sugar
3 tbsp peanut oil,
plus 3 tbsp oil, if frying the meat
20 cl unsweetened coconut milk,
or water

Preparation time: 45 minutes
(plus 1 hour's marinating time)

3,400 kJ/810 calories per portion

1 Rinse the beef or chicken briefly under cold running water, pat dry and cut into 1 cm cubes. Thread 4 cubes fairly tightly onto each skewer, leaving enough space at the blunt end to make them easy to handle while cooking. Arrange the skewers close together in a circle on a plate. Mix together the soy sauce, *kecap manis* and *sambal ulek* and spread the mixture on the meat. Leave to marinate for about 1 hour, turning from time to time.

2 Meanwhile, make the peanut sauce. Peel and finely chop the shallots and garlic. Purée the peanuts in a blender, or crush them, using a pestle and mortar. Put the shallots, garlic, peanuts, *kecap manis*, *sambal ulek*, lemon juice and sugar in a bowl and stir to form a thick paste.

3 Heat the oil in a small frying pan over medium heat and fry the peanut paste for 2 to 3 minutes. Add the coconut milk or water. Reduce the heat to low and simmer for 2 to 3 minutes, stirring constantly. If the sauce becomes too thick, add a little water.

4 Grill the skewered meat on either side for 2 to 3 minutes over a charcoal grill or for 5 to 6 minutes under a preheated grill, brushing with the remaining marinade from time to time. Alternatively, fry the meat in oil in a frying pan for about 5 minutes on each side. Divide the sauce between four plates. Arrange 10 skewers each on four plates, coat them with the peanut sauce (or serve the sauce separately in four individual bowls) and serve at once. Indonesians like to eat satay with rice in banana leaves (*page 38*).

Peanuts

Peanuts are not nuts at all. They are members of the large family of leguminous plants that include peas and lentils. Native to South America, peanuts are now grown in many parts of the world including the United States, Africa and Asia. In Indonesia, a main peanut-growing area is the island of Java.

After pollination of the flowers, most of the development of a peanut takes place below ground—hence its other name, groundnut. At harvest time, the whole plant is removed from the soil and left to dry. The nuts are marketed in their dried pods or shelled and roasted. They are also processed into oil. The little kernels are rich in vegetable fat and protein and contain fibre, vitamins A and E, and minerals.

Peanuts are much used in Indonesian cooking, especially in sauces. For the best flavour, raw peanuts can be dry roasted in a frying pan lightly rubbed with oil, and crushed just before adding to the other ingredients.

Balinese spiced beef

Daging bumbu Bali

Fairly easy • Highly spiced

Serves 4

1 walnut-sized piece compressed
tamarind pulp
750 g fillet or sirloin of beef
¼ bunch thin young spring onions,
or 1 to 2 larger ones
2 to 3 garlic cloves
4 cm piece fresh ginger
2 stalks fresh lemon grass
½ tsp terasi (see page 96)
2 to 3 tbsp coconut oil
2 tbsp kecap manis (sweet soy
sauce)
1 tsp sambal ulek (page 42)
salt

Preparation time: 40 minutes

1,200 kJ/290 calories per portion

1 Soak the tamarind pulp in 15 cl hot water and follow instructions on page 46, Step 1, top recipe.

2 While the tamarind is soaking, rinse the meat under cold running water, pat dry, then shred finely across the grain. Trim and wash the spring onions and slice diagonally into thin rings. Reserve a few green rings to use as a garnish. Peel and crush the garlic. Peel and finely grate the ginger. Trim and wash the lemon grass and finely chop the thick lower end. Crush the *terasi* with the back of a spoon.

3 Heat the oil in a wok or fireproof casserole over medium heat. Add the spring onions, lemon grass and ginger, and stir-fry for about 3 minutes until transparent, then push them to the edge of the pan. Increase the heat to high and fry the beef in batches for about 10 minutes, until browned all over.

4 Add the tamarind juice and *kecap manis* to the pan, then stir in the garlic, *terasi*, *sambal ulek* and some salt. Reduce the heat to low, cover the pan and continue to cook for a further 10 minutes. Sprinkle with the reserved spring onion rings and serve with rice and prawn crackers (*page 115*).

Meatballs with coconut

Daging rempah

Simple • Can be prepared in advance

Serves 4

500 g minced beef
½ tsp terasi (see page 96)
2 tsp palm sugar (or, if unavailable,
soft brown sugar)
4 cm piece fresh ginger
200 g desiccated coconut
½ tsp sambal ulek (page 42)
2 tsp ground coriander
1 tsp freshly ground black pepper
salt
½ litre oil for deep frying
1 red chili flower (Note, page 112)

Preparation time: 30 minutes

2,100 kJ/500 calories per portion

1 Place the minced meat in a bowl. Mix the *terasi* and sugar with 3 to 4 tbsp boiling water. Peel and grate the ginger. Add the *terasi* mixture and ginger to the meat together with the coconut, *sambal ulek*, coriander, pepper and salt. Knead everything to a paste, which should be firm enough not to stick to your fingers.

2 Shape the paste into about 30 walnut-sized balls.

3 Heat the oil in a saucepan or deep fryer. Deep fry the meatballs in batches in the oil for about 5 minutes until crisp.

4 Remove the fried meatballs with a slotted spoon and drain off the surplus fat on kitchen paper. Garnish with the chili flower and serve hot or cold, as part of a *rijstafel* (*see page 17*), with chili-tomato sauce (*page 44*).

Variation:
Meatballs with coconut milk
(*Rempah masak santen*)
Instead of deep frying the meatballs, arrange them all together in a large, shallow pan and cover them with 80 cl unsweetened coconut milk. Cover the pan and cook over low heat until the meatballs float to the surface. Remove and drain.

Javanese meatballs
Perkedel goreng Jawa

Not difficult • Substantial rijstafel dish

Serves 4

500 g sweet potatoes or floury
potatoes
salt • 4 shallots
3 garlic cloves
4 cm piece fresh ginger
¼ tsp terasi (see page 96)
500 g minced beef • 1 egg
1 tbsp kecap manis (sweet soy
sauce)
1 tsp sambal ulek (page 42)
2 tsp palm or soft brown sugar
3 tsp ground coriander
1 tsp freshly grated nutmeg
½ tsp ground cinnamon
½ litre oil for deep frying

Preparation time: 1 hour

1,700 kJ/400 calories per portion

1 Peel the potatoes and cut them into small cubes. Place them in saucepan with ¼ litre lightly salted water and bring to the boil. Reduce the heat and cook, covered, for 15 to 20 minutes until the potatoes are tender.

2 Meanwhile, peel and finely chop the shallots and garlic. Peel and finely grate the ginger. Crush the *terasi* with the back of a spoon.

3 Drain the cooked potatoes and mash them thoroughly. Leave to cool a little. Mix with the beef, egg, shallots, garlic, ginger, *terasi*, *kecap manis*, *sambal ulek*, sugar, spices and salt. The mixture should be firm enough not to stick to your fingers.

4 Shape the mixture into 28 to 32 balls about the size of a plum. Heat the oil in a deep-fryer. Fry the meatballs in batches for about 5 minutes, until crisp. Remove with a slotted spoon and drain on kitchen paper. Serve hot or cold as part of a *rijstafel*, accompanied by grated coconut with peanuts (*see below*), chili-tomato sauce (*page 44*) and prawn crackers (*page 115*).

Grated coconut with peanuts
(*Serundeng kacang*)
Dry-fry 50 g grated coconut and 50 g peanuts in a frying pan without oil for about 10 minutes over low heat, until golden-brown, stirring constantly. Stir in some palm sugar and leave to cool. If you like, the *serundeng* can be sprinkled over the meatballs.

Beef in soy sauce
Semur daging

Takes a little time • Highly-spiced

Serves 4

2 walnut-sized pieces compressed
tamarind pulp
750 g beef (sirloin or rump)
3 garlic cloves
4 cm piece fresh ginger
3 to 4 tbsp coconut or vegetable oil
salt • ½ tsp ground black pepper
1 tsp ground cardamom
1 tsp ground cinnamon
1 tsp freshly grated nutmeg
4 tsp palm or soft brown sugar
5 tbsp soy sauce
1 red chili flower (Note, page 112)

Preparation time: 1½ hours

1,300 kJ/310 calories per portion

1 Soak the tamarind pulp in ¼ litre hot water and follow instructions on page 46, Step 1, top recipe.

2 While the tamarind pulp is soaking, rinse the beef under cold running water, pat dry and cut into 2 cm cubes, removing any fat and sinews. Peel and crush the garlic. Peel and finely grate the ginger.

3 Heat the oil in a wok or fireproof casserole over medium heat and fry the garlic and ginger until transparent. Increase the heat to high, add the meat

cubes in batches and fry for about 10 minutes, until browned all over. Season with salt and pepper.

4 Add the tamarind juice, 12.5 cl water, the spices, sugar and soy sauce. Reduce the heat to low, cover the pan and cook for about 1 hour, until nearly all the sauce has evaporated. Serve on a bed of rice, garnished with the red chili flower.

Beef soup

Not difficult • Hot and spicy

Sop daging

500 g brisket of beef
1.25 litres vegetable stock
1 bunch thin young spring onions,
or 4 to 5 larger ones
3 garlic cloves
4 cm piece fresh ginger
1 to 2 tbsp coconut or vegetable oil
100 g peeled, cooked prawns
½ tsp sambal ulek (page 42)
½ tsp turmeric
juice of 1 lemon
salt

Preparation time: 1½ hours

1,000 kJ/240 calories per portion

1 Rinse the beef under cold running water, pat dry and cut into bite-sized pieces. Bring 1 litre of the vegetable stock to the boil in a large saucepan. As soon as the water bubbles, add the meat. Return to the boil, reduce the heat to low and simmer the soup for about 1 hour, removing the scum from the surface during the first 30 minutes of cooking. The meat is done when it can easily be pricked with a fork.

2 Meanwhile, trim and wash the spring onions, and cut them into 5 mm rings. Peel and crush the garlic. Peel and finely grate the ginger.

3 Heat the oil in another pan over medium heat and fry the spring onions, garlic, ginger and prawns for about 2 minutes. Add the remaining vegetable stock, *sambal ulek*, turmeric and lemon juice, and simmer for a further 3 minutes. Transfer to the meat in the first pan. Season with salt.

Variation:
Mutton soup (*Sop kambing*)
Replace the beef with mutton or lamb, and try using fresh galangal instead of the ginger.

Note: In Indonesia, soups are eaten as an accompaniment to rice.

Noodle soup with meatballs

Fairly easy • Bali   **Mie bakso**

4 shallots • 2 garlic cloves
4 cm piece fresh ginger • 2 carrots
100 g white cabbage leaves
1 red chili pepper (see Glossary)
2 tbsp vegetable oil
1.5 litres chicken stock
225 g minced beef
1 egg white • 1 tbsp cornflour
1 tsp ground coriander
freshly ground white pepper • salt
100 g thin egg noodles
1 tbsp kecap manis (sweet soy sauce)
6 tbsp crispy fried onion rings (page 28)

Preparation time: 40 minutes

1,700 kJ/400 calories per portion

1 Peel and finely chop the shallots and garlic. Peel and finely grate the ginger. Peel the carrots, and cut into thin matchsticks. Wash the cabbage leaves, shake dry, then cut into strips 1 cm wide. Wash the chili pepper, cut in half lengthwise and discard the stalk and seeds. Cut the halves diagonally into thin strips. Place the chili strips in ice-cold water and set aside for garnish.

2 Heat the oil in a large saucepan over medium heat. Fry the shallots, garlic and ginger for 2 to 3 minutes. Remove 1 tbsp of the mixture from the pan and reserve. Add the carrots and fry for about 5 minutes, then add the cabbage and fry for a further 3 minutes. Pour in the chicken stock. Stir thoroughly and return to the boil.

3 Meanwhile, place the minced meat in a bowl. Add the reserved shallot mixture, the egg white and cornflour. Season with the coriander, pepper and salt, and knead into a dough. Form the mixture into 18 to 24 walnut-sized balls.

4 When the soup comes to the boil, add the meatballs and reduce the heat to low. Simmer the meatballs for 4 to 5 minutes. Finally, add the noodles and cook until they are *al dente*. Remove the pan from the heat and season the soup with *kecap manis* and salt. Drain the chili pepper strips, sprinkle them over the soup with the crispy fried onions and serve with steamed rice.

Loin of suckling pig

More complex • Bali

Babi guling

Serves 8 to 10

6 shallots
5 garlic cloves
6 cm piece fresh ginger
2 stalks fresh lemon grass
5 cloves
½ tsp terasi (see page 96)
1 tsp sambal ulek (page 42)
1 tsp turmeric
3 tsp ground coriander
½ tsp freshly grated nutmeg
2 tsp freshly ground black pepper
4 tsp palm sugar (or, if unavailable, soft brown sugar)
1 loin of suckling pig (1.5 to 2 kg)
salt
4 tbsp coconut or vegetable oil

Preparation time: 1¼ to 1½ hours
(plus 30 minutes' cooling time)

1,700 kJ/400 calories per portion
(if serving 10)

1 Peel and finely chop the shallots and garlic. Peel and finely grate the ginger. Trim and wash the lemon grass and finely chop the thick, lower end. Using a pestle and mortar, crush the cloves. Crush the *terasi* with the back of a spoon. Put the vegetables, *terasi* and *sambal ulek* in a bowl with the spices and sugar, and mix to a thick paste.

2 Preheat the oven to 225°C (425°F or Mark 7). Wash the loin under cold running water, pat it dry, then cut a pocket in the fleshy side of the meat with a sharp knife, taking care not to break the joint into two halves. Rub the inside and outside of the meat with salt. Fill the pocket with the spicy paste (*above*).

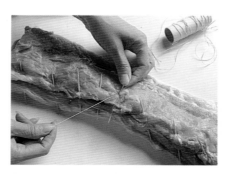

3 Secure the pocket with wooden skewers or toothpicks and wind kitchen twine diagonally crosswise round the skewers (*above*).

4 Heat the oil in a fireproof roasting pan. Lay the joint in the pan with the skewers upwards and brown over high heat for 10 to 20 minutes. Turn the joint so that the crackling is upwards, then place the pan in the centre of the oven, and roast for a further 10 to 20 minutes, basting frequently with the pan juices. To test whether the meat is cooked, prick in the thickest part with a fork or the point of a knife. If the juice runs clear, the meat is done.

5 Remove the joint from the roasting pan, and cook for a further 10 to 15 minutes under a preheated grill, until the crackling is crisp. Remove the skewers and twine, carve the meat into slices and serve on a banana leaf, accompanied, if you like, by toasted bananas (*see below*).

Toasted bananas

Cut whole bananas in half lengthwise, and toast them under a hot grill for about 5 minutes.

Note: On special family occasions or major religious festivals, the Hindu Balinese prepare small, stuffed suckling pigs, artistically decorated with fruit and flowers, to sacrifice to the gods. Since suckling pigs are rarely cooked whole here, we have used only the loin for this recipe.

Pork fillet in soy sauce

Not difficult • Bali

Babi kecap

Serves 4

750 g pork fillet
4 shallots
3 to 4 cloves garlic
4 cm piece fresh ginger or galangal
3 tbsp soy sauce
½ tsp sambal ulek (page 42)
salt
freshly ground white pepper
3 to 4 tbsp coconut or vegetable oil
5 tbsp kecap manis (sweet soy
sauce)

Preparation time: 45 minutes
(plus 1 hour's marinating time)

1,700 kJ/400 calories per portion

1 Rinse the pork fillet under cold running water, pat dry and cut across the grain into strips 1 cm wide. Peel and halve the shallots, then cut into thin slices. Peel and crush the garlic. Peel and finely grate the ginger or galangal. Place the meat, shallots, garlic and ginger in a bowl and stir in the soy sauce, *sambal ulek*, salt and pepper. Cover the bowl and marinate for at least 1 hour, until the meat has thoroughly absorbed the marinade.

2 Heat the oil in a wok or fireproof casserole over high heat. Fry the marinated meat in batches for 5 to 10 minutes until browned all over.

Reduce the heat and add the *kecap manis* and 10 cl water. Cover the pan and simmer for about 20 minutes, stirring from time to time, until the sauce thickens slightly. Serve with rice and cucumber salad (*page 115*).

Variation:
Lamb in soy sauce
(*Kambing kecap*)
Use lean lamb instead of the pork and replace the water with unsweetened coconut milk.

Sweet-and-sour pork

Fairly easy • Bali

Babi asam manis

Serves 4

1 walnut-sized piece compressed
tamarind pulp
2 large beef tomatoes
750 g lean pork
2 shallots
2 to 3 garlic cloves
4 cm piece fresh ginger
3 to 4 tbsp coconut oil
½ to 1 tsp sambal ulek (page 42)
2 tbsp soy sauce
5 tsp palm sugar (or, if unavailable,
soft brown sugar)

Preparation time: 1 hour

1,900 kJ/450 calories per portion

1 Soak the tamarind pulp in 15 cl hot water and follow instructions on page 46, Step 1, top recipe.

2 While the tamarind is soaking, briefly plunge the tomatoes in boiling water and skin them. Cut them in half, remove the seeds and finely chop the flesh. Rinse the meat under cold running water, pat dry, then cut across the grain into thin strips. Peel and halve the shallots and cut into thin slices. Peel and crush the garlic. Peel and finely grate the ginger.

3 Heat the oil in a wok or fireproof casserole over medium heat and stir-fry the shallots, garlic, ginger and *sambal ulek* for about 3 minutes. Increase the heat to high, add the meat in batches and fry for 5 to 10 minutes until browned all over. Stir in the chopped tomatoes. Add the tamarind juice. Reduce the heat to low, then add the soy sauce and sugar. Cover the pan and simmer for a further 30 to 45 minutes. Serve with rice.

Barbecued spare ribs

Iga babi bakar

Simple · Kalimantan

Serves 4

1 kg meaty pork spare ribs (ask the
butcher to chop them into serving
pieces)

salt

2 tsp freshly ground black pepper

3 garlic cloves

6 tbsp coconut or vegetable oil

5 tbsp soy sauce

3 tsp palm sugar (or, if unavailable,
soft brown sugar)

Preparation time: 45 minutes

3,400 kJ/810 calories per portion

1 Wash the spare ribs under cold running water, pat dry and sprinkle with salt and pepper. Peel and very finely chop the garlic.

2 Heat the oil in a large frying pan over medium heat. Fry the garlic for about 1 minute, until transparent. Increase the heat to high, add the spare ribs and fry them until crisp and brown all over.

3 Add 20 cl water. Stir in the soy sauce and sugar, and allow the sauce to thicken slightly. Reduce the heat to medium and cook the ribs for a further 25 to 35 minutes, adding a little more water if necessary, until the meat is very tender. The sauce should have almost completely boiled away and the meat should be glazed with the sauce.

4 Arrange the spare ribs on a banana leaf, and serve with rice.

Crispy roast chicken

Ayam panggang

Takes a little time · Highly spiced

Serves 4

1 oven-ready chicken (about 1.5 kg)

1 bunch thin young spring onions,
or 4 to 5 larger ones

4 garlic cloves

2 stalks fresh lemon grass

5 shelled kemiri or macadamia nuts

½ tsp terasi (see page 96)

½ tsp sambal ulek (page 42)

½ tsp turmeric

2 tsp ground coriander

salt

3 to 4 tbsp coconut oil

40 cl canned unsweetened coconut
milk

Preparation time: 1¼ hours

4,500 kJ/1,100 calories per portion

1 Halve the chicken by cutting along the breast bone and down the back. Wash thoroughly and pat dry. Trim and wash the spring onions and cut into thin rings. Peel and crush the garlic. Trim and wash the lemon grass and finely chop the thick, lower end. Finely grate the nuts. Crush the *terasi* with the back of a spoon.

2 Put the spring onions, garlic, lemon grass, grated nuts and *terasi* in a bowl with the *sambal ulek*, turmeric, coriander and some salt, and stir to form a thick paste. Preheat the oven to 200°C (400°F or Mark 6).

3 Heat 2 tbsp of the oil in a large sauté pan. Stir-fry the spicy paste for about 1 minute. Add the chicken halves, pour over the coconut milk, cover the pan and simmer for about 20 minutes.

4 Remove the chicken from the sauce. Pour a little of the remaining oil into a roasting pan, then rub the chicken with the rest. Place the chicken in the roasting pan, skin side up, and roast in the top of the oven for 30 to 40 minutes, until the skin is crisp and brown.

5 Meanwhile, continue to cook the sauce, uncovered, over medium heat until it begins to thicken. When the chicken is ready, divide it into serving pieces and arrange in a bowl lined with a banana leaf. Serve with rice and prawn crackers (*page 115*).

Chicken soup
Soto ayam

Serves 4

1 chicken (about 1 kg)
2 sticks celery
salt
4 eggs
2 medium-sized floury potatoes
75 g cellophane noodles
5 shallots
4 garlic cloves
4 cm piece fresh ginger
2 stalks fresh lemon grass
½ tsp terasi (see page 96)
5 shelled kemiri or macadamia nuts
juice of 1 lemon
½ tsp sambal ulek (page 42)
½ tsp turmeric
2 tsp ground coriander
200 g bean sprouts
2 tbsp coconut oil
kecap manis (sweet soy sauce)
4 tbsp crispy fried onion rings
(page 28)
strips of red chili pepper

Preparation time: about 2 hours

2,700 kJ/640 calories per portion

1 Divide the chicken into 8 pieces (*see Note, page 39*) and wash thoroughly. Trim and wash the celery, and cut into 1 cm pieces. Place the chicken pieces and celery in a large saucepan and add enough water to cover. Add salt, bring to the boil, then reduce the heat to low, cover the pan and simmer for 1 to 1¼ hours.

2 While the chicken is cooking, hard boil the eggs, plunge them into cold water, then set aside. Peel and slice the potatoes. Place them in a pan of salted water, bring to the boil, cover the pan, and simmer for 15 to 20 minutes, until tender. Drain off the water, and reserve the potatoes.

3 Place the cellophane noodles in a bowl with boiling water. Soak for about 10 minutes, drain through a colander, and cut into short pieces (*above*).

4 Peel and finely chop the shallots and garlic. Peel and finely grate the ginger. Trim and wash the lemon grass and finely chop the thick, lower end. Crush the *terasi* with the back of a spoon. Finely grate the nuts. Put the shallots, garlic, ginger, lemon grass, *terasi* and grated nuts in a bowl together with the lemon juice, *sambal ulek*, turmeric and coriander. Stir to form a thick paste.

5 Remove the chicken from the stock. Strain the broth through a sieve and reserve for later use. Remove the skin and bones from the chicken, and cut the meat into strips. Shell and slice the hard-boiled eggs. Rinse the bean sprouts under cold running water, and drain through a colander.

6 Heat the oil in a large saucepan over medium heat. Fry the spicy paste for about 3 minutes, then add 1.5 litres of the stock. Return the soup to the boil, and add the chicken, noodles and bean sprouts. Remove the pan from the heat and season the soup to taste with *kecap manis* and salt.

7 Divide the potatoes and sliced egg between four large soup bowls, ladle the soup on top, sprinkle each serving with 1 tbsp crispy fried onion rings and garnish with a chili pepper strip.

Note: Four different types of soup appear on Indonesian menus: *sayur, soto, sop* and *bakso*. If you order a *sayur*, you will be served a soup whose ingredients have been cooked in coconut milk, which gives it a unique flavour. *Soto* is a substantial, stew-like soup enriched with vegetables, meat, and rice or cellophane noodles, and often thickened with grated coconut. *Sop* is a simpler soup prepared with water, while *bakso* is a hot and spicy broth in which rice noodles, vegetables and meatballs float.

Fried chicken

Fairly easy • National dish

Ayam goreng

1 oven-ready roasting chicken,
(about 1.5 kg)
3 tbsp coconut or vegetable oil
1 red chili flower (Note, page 112)

For the marinade:
1 walnut-sized piece compressed
tamarind pulp
3 shallots
4 garlic cloves
4 cm piece fresh ginger
1 tsp sambal ulek (page 42)
2 tsp ground coriander
salt

Preparation time: 45 minutes
(plus 2 hours' marinating time)

2,400 kJ/570 calories per portion

1 Divide the chicken into 8 pieces (*see Note, page 39*), wash thoroughly and pat dry.

2 For the marinade, soak the tamarind pulp in 15 cl hot water and follow the instructions on page 46, Step 1, top recipe. While the tamarind is soaking, peel and finely chop the shallots and garlic. Peel and grate the ginger.

3 Put the tamarind juice, shallots, garlic and ginger in a bowl with the *sambal ulek*, coriander and salt, and stir well. Brush the chicken pieces with the marinade, and leave to stand in a covered dish for at least 2 hours. Remove the chicken pieces from the marinade, and drain thoroughly.

4 Heat the oil in a large frying pan over medium heat. Fry the chicken for about 10 minutes on each side until crisp and brown. To test whether the chicken is done, prick one leg with the point of a knife. The juice should run clear, not pink. Garnish with the red chili flower and serve with yellow rice (*page 28*) and cucumber slices.

Note: The chicken can also be grilled over charcoal for about 15 minutes on each side, but be careful not to place the pieces too close to the charcoal, otherwise the skin will burn. Crisply fried or grilled chicken is eaten with the fingers and is very popular all over Indonesia. The marinade, which gives the chicken its exotic flavour, varies from region to region.

Variations:

Fried chicken Javanese-style
(*Ayam goreng kuning*)
For the marinade, replace the tamarind juice with 15 cl unsweetened coconut milk, use galangal instead of ginger, and add ½ tbsp turmeric, 4 grated macadamia nuts and 2 tbsp fresh or dried grated coconut. Reserve the marinade and, after frying the chicken, pour it into the pan. Cook, uncovered, over medium heat until the sauce thickens, then spoon over the chicken.

Fried chicken Balinese-style
(*Ayam goreng Bali*)
For the marinade, replace the tamarind juice with 10 cl unsweetened coconut milk and 3 tbsp *kecap manis*. Add 3 tsp palm sugar.

Fried chicken Sumatra-style
(*Ayam bakar*)
For the marinade, replace the tamarind juice with 3 tbsp soy sauce and 3 tbsp *kecap manis*, and add 3 tsp freshly ground black pepper and 1 to 2 tsp *sambal ulek*.

Bali duck

A little more complex • A festive dish

Bebek betutu

1 banana leaf
vegetable oil
5 shallots
5 garlic cloves
12 shelled kemiri or macadamia nuts
4 cm piece fresh ginger or galangal
½ tsp terasi (see page 96)
2 blades mace
½ tsp sambal ulek (page 42)
½ tsp turmeric
½ tsp ground cardamom
2 tsp freshly ground black pepper
salt
3 tbsp coconut oil
1 oven-ready duck (1.5 to 2 kg)
strips red chili pepper
1 spring onion, green part only

Preparation time: 2½ hours

3,700 kJ/880 calories per portion
(if serving 6)

1 Plunge the banana leaf briefly into boiling water (*above*) and pat dry. Brush the inner side of the leaf with vegetable oil.

2 Peel and finely chop the shallots and garlic. Finely grate the nuts. Peel and finely grate the ginger or galangal. Crush the *terasi* and mace with the back of a spoon. Put these ingredients in a bowl with the *sambal ulek*, turmeric, cardamom, pepper and salt, and stir to form a thick paste.

3 Heat the coconut oil in a frying pan over medium heat and stir-fry the spicy paste for about 2 minutes. Remove the pan from the heat and leave to cool. Preheat the oven to 200°C (400°F or Mark 6).

4 Rinse the duck under running water, pat dry and rub inside and out with the spicy paste. Wrap the duck in the banana leaf and secure with wooden skewers (*above*) or kitchen twine. Place on a grid in a roasting pan in the centre of the oven for 1½ hours. If you like very crisp skin, remove the banana leaf for the last 10 minutes of cooking, increasing the oven temperature to 250°C (475°F or Mark 9).

5 Drain off surplus fat and carve the duck into serving pieces. Arrange them on a serving dish lined with the open banana leaf. Garnish with the red chili strips and the green part of the spring onion cut into thin strips lengthwise, and serve with yellow rice (*page 28*).

Note: The duck fat can be saved for frying meat and vegetables. Aluminium foil can replace the banana leaf.

Ducks are bred in large numbers on Bali, mainly for their eggs. On special occasions such as religious festivals—of which there are plenty, since numerous Hindu gods are still worshipped on the island—freshly killed young ducks are thickly spread with aromatic, spicy paste, and wrapped in banana leaves. They are then grilled over a pit filled with glowing charcoal, or over an open fire, using coconut shells to fan the flames.

Fried fish in batter

Quick and easy • The Moluccas

Ikan goreng

Serves 4

750 g firm-fleshed fish fillets (cod, haddock, redfish or monkfish)
salt
juice of 1 lemon
1 tbsp soy or other vegetable oil
5 tbsp flour
2 tbsp cornflour
1 tsp baking powder
½ litre coconut oil for deep frying

Preparation time: 30 minutes (plus 15 minutes' marinating time)

910 kJ/220 calories per portion

1 Rinse the fish fillets under cold running water, pat dry and cut into 5-cm pieces. Season lightly with salt, sprinkle with half the lemon juice, then leave to marinate for about 15 minutes.

2 Meanwhile, make a batter with the soy oil, flour, cornflour, baking powder and 10 tbsp hot water.

3 Heat the coconut oil in a heavy pan or deep-fryer. Remove the fish pieces from the marinade, pat dry, then dip in the batter to coat them. Deep fry the fish in batches until golden. To avoid the pieces of fish sticking together, fry only a few at a time. Remove them with a slotted spoon and drain on kitchen paper. Sprinkle with the rest of the lemon juice. Serve with rice and, if you like, tomato ketchup.

Variations:
Fried prawns in batter
(*Udang goreng*)
Instead of fish fillets, use 500 g of peeled, cooked prawns. Rinse them under cold running water and pat dry before coating with batter.

Fried squid in batter
(*Cumi cumi goreng*)
Instead of fish fillets, use cleaned, ready-to-cook small squid. Wash and dry them thoroughly. Halve each squid pouch lengthwise, then cut into bite-sized pieces; the tentacles can be fried in the same way.

Note: The fish can be fried in vegetable oil instead of the coconut oil, but the taste will be slightly different.

Red mullet in coconut sauce

Not difficult • Sulawesi

Ikan bumbu santen

Serves 4

4 red mullet, each weighing about 250 g, cleaned and ready to cook
salt • 4 shallots
3 garlic cloves
4 cm piece fresh ginger
2 stalks fresh lemon grass
6 tbsp coconut oil
plus 2 tbsp for the sauce
½ tsp sambal ulek (page 42)
¼ litre canned unsweetened coconut milk
2 tsp palm or soft brown sugar

Preparation time: 35 minutes

2,700 kJ/640 calories per portion

1 Remove the heads and fins from the fish. Rinse thoroughly under cold running water and pat dry with kitchen paper. Sprinkle with salt.

2 Peel and very finely chop the shallots and garlic. Peel and finely grate the ginger. Trim and wash the lemon grass and finely chop the thick, lower end.

3 Heat the oil in a frying pan over medium heat. Fry the fish, in 2 batches if necessary, for about 5 minutes on each side. Arrange on a warmed serving dish and keep warm.

4 In the remaining oil in the pan, fry the shallots, garlic, ginger, lemon grass and *sambal ulek* for about 2 minutes. Add the coconut milk and sugar, and bring briefly to the boil. Pour the sauce over the fish and serve with rice.

Note: Other firm-fleshed fish can be cooked in the same way.

Fish in soy sauce
Ikan kecap

Fairly easy • Sumatra

Serves 4

1 walnut-sized piece compressed tamarind pulp
750 g firm-fleshed fish fillets (cod, redfish, haddock, monkfish or tuna)
salt
½ bunch thin young spring onions, or 2 to 3 larger ones
2 garlic cloves
4 cm piece fresh ginger
3 to 4 tbsp coconut or vegetable oil
3 tbsp soy sauce
3 tbsp kecap manis (sweet soy sauce)
½ tsp sambal ulek (page 42)
5 sprigs fresh coriander
freshly ground black pepper

Preparation time: 35 minutes

910 kJ/220 calories per portion

1 Soak the tamarind pulp in 15 cl hot water and follow the instructions on page 46, Step 1, top recipe.

2 While the tamarind is soaking, rinse the fish fillets under cold running water, pat dry and cut into 15 mm pieces. Season lightly with salt.

3 Trim and wash the spring onions, cut them into 5 cm-long pieces, then into strips. Set the green parts aside for garnish. Peel and crush the garlic. Peel and finely grate the ginger.

4 Heat the oil in a wok or fireproof casserole over high heat. Fry the fish in batches for 3 to 5 minutes, until browned all over. Remove from the pan and keep warm.

5 Add the white spring onion strips, garlic and ginger to the pan and stir-fry for about 1 minute. Add the tamarind juice. Season with both soy sauces and *sambal ulek*, and continue to stir-fry until the sauce has thickened slightly.

6 Reduce the heat to low and carefully place the fish pieces in the sauce. Cover the pan and simmer for a further 2 to 3 minutes. Sprinkle with the green onion strips and fresh coriander. Season to taste with pepper and salt, and serve with rice.

Baked spiced mackerel
Ikan pepes

Not difficult • Kalimantan

Serves 4

1 large banana leaf
4 mackerel, each weighing 250 to 300 g, cleaned and ready to cook
2 fresh red chili peppers (see Glossary)
3 garlic cloves
6 tbsp kecap manis (sweet soy sauce)
juice of ½ lemon
3 tsp palm sugar (or, if unavailable, soft brown sugar)
salt
vegetable oil

Preparation time: 35 minutes (plus 30 minutes' marinating time)

2,000 kJ/480 calories per portion

1 Wipe the banana leaf clean with a damp cloth or plunge it briefly into boiling water and pat dry.

2 Rinse the mackerel thoroughly, pat dry, then make diagonal incisions on both sides, to absorb maximum flavour from the marinade. Wash the chili peppers, cut in half lengthwise and discard the stalks and seeds. Cut the halves into thin strips. Peel and crush the garlic.

3 In a bowl, stir together the chili peppers, garlic, *kecap manis*, lemon juice, sugar and some salt. Spread it over the insides and outsides of the fish and leave to marinate for about 30 minutes. Meanwhile light a charcoal grill or preheat an ordinary grill. Alternatively, preheat the oven to 180°C (350°F or Mark 4).

4 Cut the banana leaf into four rectangles, large enough to wrap the fish, and brush the inner sides with a little vegetable oil. Wrap each mackerel in a rectangle.

5 Grill the parcels for 15 minutes each side over charcoal embers, or for 25 minutes under a preheated grill. Alternatively, bake in the centre of the oven for about 25 minutes. The banana leaves are not edible, but give a special flavour to the fish.

Sweet-and-sour fish

Ikan asam manis

Not difficult • Java

Serves 4

1 walnut-sized piece compressed tamarind pulp
750 g firm-fleshed fish fillets (cod, redfish, haddock, monkfish or tuna)
salt
½ bunch thin young spring onions, or 2 to 3 larger ones
2 garlic cloves
4 cm piece fresh ginger
3 to 4 tbsp coconut or vegetable oil
½ to 1 tsp sambal ulek (page 42)
4 tbsp tomato ketchup
5 tsp palm sugar (or, if unavailable, soft brown sugar)
chili-tomato sauce (page 44)

Preparation time: 30 minutes

1,000 kJ/240 calories per portion

1 Soak the tamarind pulp in 15 cl hot water and follow the instructions on page 46, Step 1, top recipe.

2 While the tamarind is soaking, rinse the fish fillets under cold running water, pat dry and cut into 2 cm cubes. Sprinkle with salt. Trim and wash the spring onions and cut them diagonally into thin rings. Peel and crush the garlic. Peel and finely grate the ginger.

3 Heat the oil in a wok or frying pan over high heat, and fry the fish cubes in batches for 2 to 3 minutes until browned all over. Remove the fish from the pan and keep warm.

4 Stir-fry the spring onions, garlic and ginger in the remaining oil for 2 to 3 minutes until transparent. Add the tamarind juice, then the *sambal ulek*, tomato ketchup and sugar. Reduce the heat to low and simmer the sauce for about 5 minutes. Place the fish in the sauce and continue to simmer for a further 2 to 3 minutes. Serve with rice and the chili-tomato sauce.

Variation:
Sweet-and-sour prawns
(*Udang asam manis*)
Instead of fish, use 500 g peeled, cooked prawns. About 1 minute before the end of the cooking time, add 100 g rinsed bean sprouts.

Sea bass baked in banana leaf

Fairly easy • Sulawesi **Ikan panggang** *Serves 4*

1 large banana leaf
1 walnut-sized piece compressed tamarind pulp
1 sea bass (or grey mullet or gilt-head bream), about 1 kg, cleaned and ready to cook
2 shallots
3 garlic cloves
4 cm piece fresh ginger
5 sprigs fresh coriander
1 tbsp kecap manis (sweet soy sauce)
2 tsp sambal ulek (page 42)
½ tsp turmeric
2 tsp ground coriander
salt
vegetable oil

Preparation time: 1 hour

860 kJ/200 calories per portion

1 Wipe the banana leaf clean with a damp cloth or plunge it briefly into boiling water and pat dry. Preheat the oven to 200°C (400°F or Mark 6). Soak the tamarind pulp in 15 cl hot water and follow instructions on page 46, Step 1, top recipe.

2 While the tamarind is soaking, rinse the fish thoroughly under cold running water and pat dry. Make diagonal incisions about 1 cm apart along both sides of the fish, to absorbs maximum flavour from the seasonings. Peel and finely chop the shallots and garlic. Peel and finely grate the ginger. Wash the coriander, shake dry and chop finely.

3 Put the shallots, garlic, ginger, fresh and ground coriander and the tamarind juice into a bowl with the *kecap manis*,

sambal ulek, turmeric and some salt. Stir together to form a paste. Spread some of the paste over both sides of the fish, stuffing the body cavity with the remainder. Brush the inner side of the banana leaf with a little vegetable oil. Wrap the fish in the leaf and secure with wooden skewers.

4 Pour a little oil into the roasting pan. Arrange the fish in the pan, and bake in the centre of the oven for 30 to 50 minutes. Serve the fish wrapped in the banana leaf and unwrap at the table.

Note: Aluminium foil can be used instead of the banana leaf. To make sure the fish is cooked, open one end of the parcel and with a fork lift a little of the flesh. If it comes away easily from the bone, it is done.

Fish paté
Otak otak

A little more complex • Java

Serves 4

1 large banana leaf
500 g firm-fleshed fish fillets (cod, redfish, haddock, monkfish or tuna)
250 g peeled, cooked prawns
salt
4 fresh red chili peppers (see Glossary)
½ bunch thin young spring onions, or 2 to 3 larger ones
4 garlic cloves
2 stalks fresh lemon grass
2 tsp ground coriander
10 cl canned unsweetened coconut milk
vegetable oil • 1 lime

Preparation time: 1 hour

2,000 kJ/480 calories per portion

1 Wipe the banana leaf clean with a damp cloth or plunge it briefly into boiling water and pat dry. Rinse the fish and prawns under cold running water and pat dry, then sprinkle with salt. Wash the chili peppers, cut them in half lengthwise and discard the seeds and stalks. Cut the halves into thin strips. Trim and wash the spring onions, and cut them into thin rings. Peel and crush the garlic. Trim and wash the lemon grass and finely chop the thick, lower end. Preheat the oven to 200°C (400°F or Mark 6).

2 Put the fish, prawns, chilies, spring onions, garlic, lemon grass, ground coriander and coconut milk in a food processor or blender and purée. Cut the banana leaf into four rectangles, each about 20 by 30 cm. Brush the inner sides with a little vegetable oil. Divide the fish mixture between the four pieces of banana leaf. Fold into rectangular parcels and secure with wooden skewers.

3 Bake the parcels in the centre of the oven for 25 to 30 minutes, turning once. Alternatively, grill them for 10 minutes on either side over charcoal, or place in a bamboo or metal steamer and steam over boiling water for about 15 minutes. Serve hot or cold in the banana leaf wrapping, garnished with the lime, cut into wedges.

Spiced prawn balls
Udang rempah

Fairly easy • West Java

Serves 4

1 small leek
3 cloves garlic
4 cm piece fresh ginger
250 g peeled, cooked prawns
250 g bean sprouts
1 tomato
1 egg
100 g flour
1 tsp baking powder
½ tsp sambal ulek (page 42)
salt
½ litre oil for deep frying
1 red chili flower (Note, page 112)

Preparation time: 45 minutes

730 kJ/170 calories per portion

1 Trim the leek, cut in half lengthwise and wash. Cut the halves into strips, then chop into very small dice. Peel and crush the garlic. Peel and finely grate the ginger. Rinse the prawns under cold running water and pat dry. Rinse the bean sprouts and drain through a colander. Chop the prawns and bean sprouts very finely. Cut the tomato into slices and set aside.

2 Lightly whisk the egg in a bowl. Sift the flour and baking powder into the beaten egg. Add the prepared leek, garlic, ginger, prawns and bean sprouts to the bowl with the *sambal ulek* and some salt. Knead everything together into a dough. If the dough is too firm, add a little water, a spoonful at a time. Shape the dough into about 24 walnut-sized balls.

3 Heat the oil in a heavy pan or deep-fryer until very hot. Deep-fry the prawn balls in batches for 3 to 5 minutes, until crisp. Remove with a slotted spoon onto kitchen paper to absorb the surplus fat. Serve hot or cold as part of a *rijstafel*, garnished with the red chili flower and the sliced tomato.

VEGETABLES AND TOFU

T he fertile volcanic soil of the Indonesian islands nourishes not only many exotic native vegetables but also a wealth of others from Europe, introduced by the Dutch colonists in the 16th century. Many of the latter are still known by their Dutch names—cabbage (*kol*), beans (*buncis*), carrots (*wortel*) and tomatoes (*tomat*), for example.

Other vegetables reflect the strong Chinese influence on Indonesian cuisine. Spinach (*bayam*), aubergines (*terung)* and cucumbers (*ketimun*) are often cultivated alongside the paddy fields. Soy beans are used to make tofu (*tahu*) and *tempeh*, a fermented soy bean cake—unique to Indonesia.

This immense array of vegetables, both local and of foreign origin, has been utilized by Indonesian cooks to create many imaginative and delicious dishes. The Indonesians also conjure up delicious tidbits from vegetables, which can be bought in any of the numerous markets and from street vendors. They can be eaten as between-meal snacks or served as appetizers, and no *rijsttafel* is complete without them.

Spicy fruit salad
Rujak

Not difficult • Sumatra

Serves 6

1 walnut-sized piece compressed tamarind pulp
¼ tsp terasi (see Box, below)
1 mango
1 grapefruit or orange
½ fresh pineapple
1 small cucumber
3 apples
1 tsp sambal ulek (page 42)
3 tbsp kecap manis (sweet soy sauce)
100 g palm sugar (or, if unavailable, soft brown sugar)

Preparation time: 25 minutes

970 kJ/230 calories per portion

1 Put the tamarind pulp in a bowl with 15 cl hot water and leave to soak for about 10 minutes, then knead thoroughly to produce a thick juice. Discard any hard bits or seeds and strain through a sieve. Press the *terasi* with the back of a spoon and stir it into the tamarind juice.

2 While the tamarind is soaking, peel the mango, remove the stone and dice the flesh. Peel the grapefruit or orange, divide into segments and remove pith and membranes. Peel the pineapple half, remove the hard core and dice the flesh. Peel the cucumber, cut in half lengthwise and remove the seeds. Slice the cucumber halves, then cut into strips. Peel, core and slice the apples. Place all the ingredients in a bowl.

3 Stir the *sambal ulek*, *kecap manis* and sugar into the tamarind juice and *terasi* mixture. Pour this dressing over the fruit and stir thoroughly. Serve as an accompaniment to hot curries.

Note: Keep the other half of the pineapple cut side down on a plate. It will retain its colour and freshness for 2 to 3 days.

Terasi

Fish and seafood are an important source of protein in Southeast Asia. However, since it soon spoils in the tropical climate and is difficult to transport, various ways of drying fish have evolved over the centuries, such as sun-drying prawns and shrimps and processing fish and other seafood into concentrated pastes and sauces.

In Indonesia they make a firm paste with a strong flavour and a powerful smell called *terasi,* which is an important flavouring in a wide range of dishes, from sambals, curries and fried rice to spicy dressings for fruit salad (*recipe, above*). Made from fish off-cuts and small shellfish finely crushed with salt, it could be termed a waste product and is similar to the shrimp pastes of Malaysia (*blachan*) and Thailand (*gapi*).

Terasi is available as a thick pungent paste sold in jars or cans, or as a dry compressed block that is milder than the paste. Only the smallest amounts are needed, but the actual quantity is a matter of personal taste: it is best to start with very little and add more if required. Once opened, keep the *terasi* refrigerated and—since it has a very strong smell—well wrapped.

Vegetables with peanut sauce

Takes a little time • National dish

Gado gado

Serves 6

1 small cauliflower
½ small white cabbage
2 large waxy potatoes
300 g green beans
salt
200 g bean sprouts
6 eggs
1 small cucumber

For the peanut sauce:
2 shallots
3 garlic cloves
200 g roasted peanuts
4 tbsp kecap manis (sweet soy sauce)
juice of ½ lemon
1 tsp sambal ulek (page 42)
3 tsp palm sugar (or, if unavailable, soft brown sugar)
3 tbsp peanut oil
20 cl canned unsweetened coconut milk or vegetable cooking liquid (see Step 6)

Preparation time: 1 hour

2,400 kJ/570 calories per portion

1 Trim the cauliflower, removing the leaves and stalk. Wash, and divide into bite-sized florets. Remove outer leaves from the white cabbage, cut it in half, remove the tough stalks and ribs, and wash. Cut into strips about 1 cm wide. Peel, wash and thinly slice the potatoes. Wash and trim the beans, then cut diagonally into 4 cm pieces.

2 Bring plenty of salted water to the boil in a large saucepan. Place the cauliflower in the pan, return to the boil, then reduce the heat to medium, cover the pan and cook for about 10 minutes, or until tender but still crisp.

3 Meanwhile, bring a second pan of salted water to the boil, add the sliced potatoes, reduce the heat to medium, cover, and cook for about 10 minutes. Add the beans and cook for a further 10 minutes, until tender but still crisp.

4 Remove the cauliflower florets from the water with a slotted spoon. Return the cauliflower water to a brisk boil, add the white cabbage and cook for 3 to 5 minutes, then remove from the pan. Pour the boiling water over the bean sprouts, then drain in a colander.

6 Drain the cooked potatoes and beans through a large colander, reserving the cooking water if you wish to use it for the peanut sauce.

5 While the vegetables are cooking, hard boil the eggs, then plunge them into cold water and set aside.

7 For the peanut sauce, peel and coarsely chop the shallots. Peel the garlic. Put the shallots and garlic in a blender with the peanuts, *kecap manis*, lemon juice, *sambal ulek* and sugar and blend into a purée. Heat the oil in a frying pan over medium heat and briefly

fry the peanut purée. Reduce the heat to low, then add the coconut milk or 20 cl vegetable cooking liquid, and simmer for about 2 minutes, stirring constantly. If the sauce becomes too thick, add a little vegetable stock.

8 Peel the cucumber, cut it in half, remove the seeds and cut into thin slices. Shell the hard-boiled eggs and cut them into quarters.

9 Arrange the drained vegetables on six plates. Garnish with the sliced cucumber and eggs. Pour the peanut sauce over the salad. Serve while still warm, either on its own or with rice.

Variation:
Deep-fried tofu or *tempeh* (*see Box, page 118*) can be added to the other ingredients. Cut a piece (about 250 g) of tofu or *tempeh* in half lengthwise, then into slices about 1 cm thick. Heat ¼ litre coconut oil in a large frying pan over medium heat. Fry the slices in

batches until brown and crisp. The tofu needs about 5 minutes on either side, the *tempeh* 2 to 3 minutes. Remove from the pan with a slotted spoon onto kitchen paper to drain. Serve with the vegetables and peanut sauce as described in the main recipe.

Note: The less the vegetables are cooked, the more vitamins will be retained. *Gado gado* is even healthier served with tofu or *tempeh*, as soy beans have a high vitamin content.

Vegetable salad with coconut

Urap

Serves 6

1 walnut-sized piece compressed tamarind pulp
300 g green beans
salt
250 g bean sprouts
1 small Chinese cabbage (about 500 g)
1 small cucumber
1 onion
4 tomatoes
420 g can (210 g drained weight) baby sweetcorn

For the coconut sauce:
1 small fresh coconut
2 garlic cloves
4 cm piece fresh ginger
3 tbsp coconut oil
½ tsp sambal ulek (page 42)
2 tsp palm sugar (or, if unavailable, soft brown sugar)

Preparation time: about 1 hour

1,400 kJ/330 calories per portion

1 Soak the tamarind pulp in 15 cl hot water and follow instructions on page 46, Step 1, top recipe.

2 While the tamarind is soaking, wash and trim the beans and cut them diagonally into pieces about 4 cm long. In a saucepan, bring 1 litre salted water to the boil. Add the beans, cover the pan and boil briskly for 5 to 7 minutes. Using a slotted spoon, remove from the water and drain them in a colander. Return the water in the pot to the boil. Add the bean sprouts, boil for about 1 minute, then drain.

3 Preheat the oven to its lowest setting. Trim and wash the Chinese cabbage and cut into strips about 5 mm wide—if the cabbage is still wet, dry it in a salad spinner. Peel and halve the cucumber, then slice thinly or cut into small cubes. Peel, halve and finely slice the onion. Wash and chop the tomatoes. Briefly rinse the baby corn under running water, then drain through a colander. Place all the salad ingredients in a large bowl.

4 Using a skewer or small screwdriver, pierce through the three "eyes" under the beard of the coconut (*above*). Drain off the coconut liquid, then lay the coconut on a cloth. Using a hammer or the blunt side of a cleaver, hit the coconut shell just above the "eyes" while slowly rotating the coconut, until it cracks. Chop into several pieces.

5 Place the coconut pieces in the centre of the oven. After about 10 minutes, the coconut flesh can be easily prised from the shell with the point of a knife (*above*). Peel off the brown skin with a kitchen knife or potato peeler, then grate the coconut flesh with a coarse grater.

6 Peel and crush the garlic. Peel and finely grate the ginger.

7 Heat the oil in a frying pan over medium heat. Add the garlic and ginger and fry until transparent. Add the grated coconut, and stir-fry for about 3 minutes. Pour in the tamarind juice. Add the *sambal ulek* and sugar. Bring briefly to the boil and season with salt. Stir the sauce into the vegetables. Serve on a bed of rice in a dish lined with a banana leaf.

Stir-fried vegetables

Cap cay goreng

Not difficult • National dish

Serves 4

1 escalope of veal or pork
2 tbsp peeled, cooked prawns
1 medium-sized courgette
1 small leek
300 g white cabbage leaves
300 g fresh, or frozen, green beans
3 cloves garlic
4 cm piece fresh ginger
4 to 5 tbsp coconut or vegetable oil
1 tbsp cornflour
3 tbsp soy sauce
salt
freshly ground black pepper

Preparation time: 45 minutes

950 kJ/230 cal per portion

1 Wash the meat and pat dry. Using a very sharp knife, cut the meat across the grain into thin strips. Briefly rinse the prawns under cold running water and pat dry.

2 Trim and wash the vegetables. Top-and-tail the courgette, cut in half lengthwise and slice thinly. Cut the leek diagonally into rings. Cut the white cabbage leaves into strips. Cut the beans diagonally into pieces about 4 cm long. Peel and crush the garlic. Peel and finely grate the ginger.

3 Heat the oil in a wok or fireproof casserole. Add the meat to the pan a little at a time and stir-fry for about 2 minutes until browned all over. Add the prawns and continue to fry for a further 1 minute. Remove the meat and prawns from the pan. Fry the garlic

and ginger until transparent. Stir in the fresh beans, if using, and continue to cook for 5 to 10 minutes. Add the courgette, leek, cabbage and thawed frozen beans, if using, and continue to stir-fry for a further 5 minutes. Add 30 cl water and stir thoroughly. When the vegetables are hot, reduce the heat to low, cover the pan and cook for a further 5 minutes.

4 Mix the cornflour with 3 tbsp water and stir into the vegetables together with the soy sauce. Simmer briefly, stirring constantly, to bind the sauce. Season with salt and pepper. Serve warm with rice.

Note: Served in practically every restaurant in Indonesia, *cap cay goreng* is the local version of Chinese chop suey.

Fried cabbage omelette

Dadar telur

Simple • Inexpensive and filling

Serves 4

1 bunch thin young spring onions, or 4 to 5 larger ones
4 garlic cloves
4 cm piece fresh ginger
1 small Chinese or white cabbage
4 eggs • salt
2 to 3 tbsp coconut oil
1½ tsp sambal ulek (page 42)
4 tbsp kecap manis (sweet soy sauce)

Preparation time: 20 minutes

780 kJ/190 calories per portion

1 Trim and wash the spring onions, and cut them diagonally into thin rings. Peel and crush the garlic. Peel and finely grate the ginger. Trim the cabbage, cut it into quarters, remove the hard core or stalk, then wash and dry. Cut the quarters into strips about 5 mm wide.

2 Break the eggs into a bowl, add some salt and whisk thoroughly.

3 Heat the oil in a wok or fireproof casserole over high heat. Fry the spring onions, garlic and ginger for about 1 minute, until transparent. Add the cabbage and stir-fry for about 3 minutes. Add about 4 tbsp water, reduce the heat, cover the pan and continue to cook for a further 3 minutes. Stir in the *sambal ulek* and *kecap manis*. Pour the beaten eggs over the cabbage and continue to cook until the eggs begin to set. Serve with rice.

Stuffed pancakes

Martabak

For the dough:
300 g flour
1 egg
½ tsp salt
4 to 5 tbsp vegetable oil

For the filling:
½ bunch thin young spring onions,
or 2 to 3 larger ones
4 shallots
2 garlic cloves
15 cl vegetable oil
200 g minced beef
½ to 1 tsp sambal ulek (page 42)
salt
1 egg
1 red chili flower (Note, page 112)

**Preparation time: 45 minutes
(plus 2 hours' resting time)**

2,100 kJ/500 calories per portion

1 Mix the flour, egg, salt, 4 tbsp oil and 15 cl lukewarm water to a soft dough in a mixing bowl. Then vigorously knead it on a work surface for a few minutes more, to make a pliable dough. If it is still too sticky, grease your hands and the work surface with a little oil and continue to knead briefly. Shape the dough into a ball, brush with a little oil, cover with a cloth and leave to rest for at least 2 hours.

2 Meanwhile, to make the filling, trim and wash the spring onions and cut into thin rings. Peel and finely chop the shallots and garlic.

3 Heat 2 tbsp of the oil in a frying pan. Fry the spring onions, shallots and garlic until transparent. Add the minced meat and fry over a medium heat for about 5 minutes. Season with *sambal ulek* and salt. Remove the pan from the heat and let the mixture cool a little before stirring in the egg.

4 Divide the dough into four equal-sized pieces and shape into balls. Flatten each ball with your hand, then carefully stretch it until it is about the size of an A4 sheet of paper. The pancakes should be paper thin. Avoid splitting them.

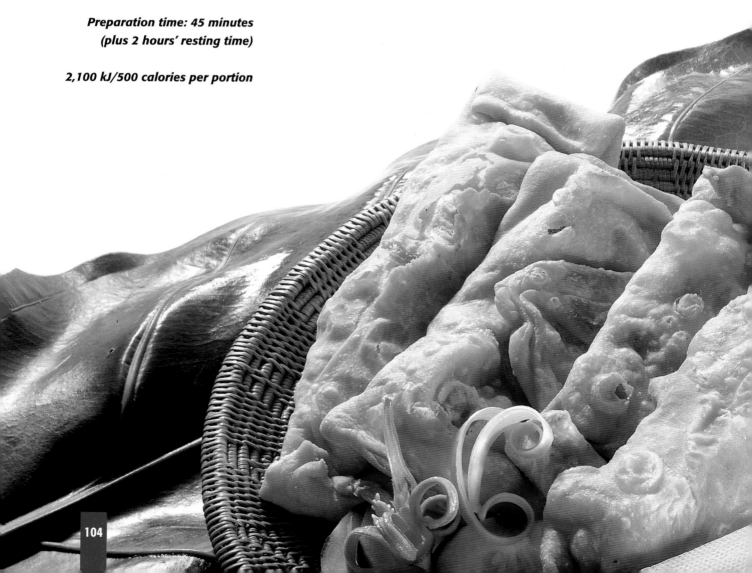

5 Place a quarter of the filling in the middle of each pancake. Fold the dough like an envelope over the filling. Heat the remaining oil in a large frying pan. Place the pancakes in the frying pan, in two batches if necessary, and press them flat (they should be about 3 cm thick). Fry over a low to medium heat for 4 to 5 minutes on each side until crisp and brown. Serve garnished with the chili flower, accompanied by crispy fried onion rings (*page 28*), slices of cucumber and tomato ketchup.

Variation:
Fried flatbread (*Roti*)
You can use the *martabak* dough on its own, without the filling, to make fried flatbread. Prepare the dough as described above, then roll it into 4 to 6 round, flat pancakes. Fry them in 12.5 cl oil in a frying pan over a medium heat for about 3 minutes on each side. These *roti* are served with curry. You tear them apart with your hands and dunk them in the sauce.

Note: *Martabak*—pronounced "mahtabah"—originated in India. These fried pancakes are now a favourite snack throughout Southeast Asia, wherever there is an Indian community, stuffed with either a sweet or, more often, a savoury filling. Once you have seen the skill and speed with which the *martabak* vendors in the night-markets of West Sumatra make the dough, you may find it hard to believe you can prepare excellent *martabak* at home. Like Italian pizza-bakers, the *martabak* sellers spin the dough through the air to create paper-thin pancakes. Truly authentic *martabak* are served wrapped in newspaper.

Indonesian spring rolls

More complex • Java and Bali

Lumpia

Makes 12 spring rolls

For the dough:
1 egg
½ tsp salt
175 g flour
rice flour for rolling out

For the filling:
60 g cellophane noodles
200 g boned chicken breast
5 Chinese cabbage leaves
1 bunch thin young spring onions,
or 4 to 5 larger ones
1 carrot
3 garlic cloves
4 cm piece fresh ginger
100 g bean sprouts
2 tbsp coconut oil
½ tsp sambal ulek (page 42)
2 tbsp kecap manis (sweet
soy sauce)
salt
½ litre oil for deep frying

Preparation time: 1 hour
(plus 3 hours' resting time)

For serving:
chili sauces (pages 42 and 44)

720 kJ/170 calories per roll

1 To make the dough for the wrappers, mix the egg and salt in a bowl with 5 tbsp water, sift in the flour, then knead to a smooth dough. Cover, and leave to rest for at least 3 hours.

2 Meanwhile, place the cellophane noodles in a bowl, pour in enough boiling water to cover and leave to soak for about 10 minutes. Rinse the chicken breast under cold running water, pat dry and dice finely. Wash the cabbage leaves, shake dry and cut them into thin strips. Trim and wash the spring onions and cut them into thin rings. Peel the carrot and cut it into matchsticks. Peel and crush the garlic. Peel and finely grate the ginger. Rinse the bean sprouts and drain thoroughly. Drain the cellophane noodles through a colander, rinse under cold running water, then chop small.

3 Heat the 2 tbsp coconut oil in a large frying pan over medium heat and fry the garlic and ginger until transparent. Increase the heat to high, add the diced chicken and stir-fry for 1 to 2 minutes. Add the spring onions and carrot, fry for about 2 minutes, then stir in the Chinese cabbage. After another 2 minutes, add the cellophane noodles, bean sprouts and *sambal ulek*, and stir-fry for a further minute. Season with *kecap manis* and salt. Remove the mixture from the heat and leave to cool.

4 Break off walnut-sized pieces of dough. On a work surface generously sprinkled with rice flour, roll the pieces to make paper-thin wrappers (*above*).

5 Put 1 tbsp of filling at the lower end of each wrapper. Fold the sides over (*above*). Brush the edges with a little water. Starting at the lower end, roll up tightly so that the filling does not trickle out. Lay the finished spring rolls on a well-floured plate.

6 Heat the ½ litre oil in a wide pan or deep-fryer until very hot. Fry the spring rolls in batches for about 5 minutes, until golden. Remove and drain on kitchen paper. Serve with chili sauces.

Variation: Instead of chicken, use peeled, cooked prawns or minced beef.

Note: Spring roll wrappers are also available ready-made from Asian food stores and some supermarkets.

Sour vegetable soup

Not difficult • Substantial **Sayur asam** *Serves 4*

4 walnut-size pieces compressed tamarind pulp
1 medium-sized aubergine
1 courgette
5 white cabbage leaves
150 g green beans
1 medium-sized floury potato
½ bunch thin young spring onions, or 2 to 3 large ones
2 to 3 garlic cloves
4 cm piece fresh ginger
4 shelled kemiri or macadamia nuts
½ tsp terasi (see page 96)
½ tsp sambal ulek (page 42)
1 tsp palm or soft brown sugar • salt
1 tbsp kecap manis (sweet soy sauce • optional)

Preparation time: 45 minutes

470 kJ/110 calories per portion

1 Soak the tamarind pulp in ¾ litre hot water and follow the instructions on page 46, Step 1, top recipe.

2 While the tamarind is soaking, wash the vegetables. Dice the aubergine. Top-and-tail and slice the courgette. Cut the white cabbage leaves into 1 cm strips. Trim the beans and cut them diagonally into pieces about 4 cm long. Peel the potato and cut it into very thin slices. Trim the spring onions and cut the white parts into thin rings, and the green parts into pieces about 5 cm long, then lengthwise into thin strips. Peel and crush the garlic. Peel and finely grate the ginger. Finely grate the nuts. Crush the *terasi* with the back of a spoon.

3 Bring the tamarind juice to the boil in a large saucepan. Cook the potatoes and beans in the juice for about 5 minutes. Add the aubergine, courgette, cabbage, white spring onion rings, garlic, ginger, grated nuts, *terasi*, *sambal ulek* and sugar. Cover the pan and cook over medium heat until the vegetables are tender but still crisp. Finally, stir in the green spring onion strips. Season with salt and, if you like, sweet soy sauce.

Note: In Indonesia, soups, which are often more like stews, are served as an accompaniment to rice.

Kemiri nuts

Kemiri are the nuts of a tree found mainly in the Moluccas—its Latin name is *Aleurites mollucana*—although on other Indonesian islands they line the streets, providing welcome shade. The nuts looks like hazelnuts, but rounder and almost as large as a walnut. Shelling them is difficult, because the shells are extremely hard and firmly attached to the kernels, so they are best bought already shelled.

The kernels are waxy and rich in oil; wrapped in banana leaf fibres they make rudimentary candles, which is why they are also known as candlenuts. Finely-grated, *kemiri* are used in Indonesian cuisine to thicken curries and soups, and to add flavour to meat, poultry and fish dishes. *Kemiri* originally came from Australia, where the closest equivalent—macadamia, or Queensland, nuts—grow. They are more easily obtainable in Europe and make a good substitute.

Vegetables in coconut milk
Sayur lodeh

Not difficult • Java and Bali

Serves 4

1 courgette
5 white cabbage leaves
¼ cauliflower • 1 carrot
1 sweet yellow pepper
½ bunch thin young spring onions,
or 2 to 3 larger ones
100 g bean sprouts
1 small can bamboo shoots
1 shallot • 3 cloves garlic
4 shelled kemiri or macadamia nuts
½ tsp terasi (see page 96)
½ tsp sambal ulek (page 42)
salt • 1 to 2 tbsp coconut oil
40 cl canned unsweetened
coconut milk
freshly ground black pepper
1 tbsp kecap manis (optional)

Preparation time: 45 minutes

2,400 kJ/570 calories per portion

1 Wash and top-and-tail the courgette, cut in half lengthwise and slice. Wash the cabbage leaves and cut into strips about 1 cm wide. Trim and wash the cauliflower and separate into small florets. Peel and dice the carrot. Wash the sweet pepper, halve and deseed, and remove ribs and stalk, then cut into strips. Trim and wash the spring onions, cut into 5 cm-long pieces, then into strips. Rinse the bean sprouts and bamboo shoots under running water and drain through a colander; cut the bamboo shoots into strips.

2 Peel and finely chop the shallot and garlic. Finely grate the nuts. Crush the terasi with the back of a spoon. Put the shallot, garlic, nuts and terasi in a bowl with the sambal ulek and salt and stir to form a thick paste.

3 Heat the oil in a wok or heavy pan over medium heat and stir-fry the paste for about 3 minutes, then stir in 20 cl water and the coconut milk. Add the vegetables, reduce the heat to low, cover the pan and simmer for 10 to 15 minutes until tender. Season with salt and pepper and, if you like, kecap manis. Serve with rice.

Note: Sayur denotes a soup—often substantial, as here—made with coconut milk. Most vegetables are suitable for this dish, but should be cooked for only a short time in the coconut milk to ensure that the ingredients retain their colour, texture and flavour.

Spinach soup
Bobor bayam

Not difficult • Java

Serves 4

500 g fresh leaf spinach
1 small leek
½ bunch thin young spring onions,
or 2 to 3 larger ones
3 garlic cloves
4 cm piece fresh ginger
340 g can sweetcorn
2 tbsp coconut oil
40 cl canned unsweetened
coconut milk
½ tsp sambal ulek (page 42)
freshly grated nutmeg • salt

Preparation time: 40 minutes

3,400 kJ/810 calories per portion

1 Thoroughly wash the spinach, remove stems and hard ribs, and coarsely chop. Trim and wash the leek and spring onions, then cut diagonally into thin rings. Peel and crush the garlic. Peel and finely grate the ginger. Rinse the sweetcorn under running water and drain.

2 Heat the oil in a wok or heavy pan over medium heat. Fry the leek, spring onions, garlic and ginger for about 3 minutes. Add the spinach with the water still clinging to it, and fry until it wilts. Pour in the coconut milk. Stir in the sweetcorn and sambal ulek, reduce the heat to low and simmer for about 5 minutes. Season to taste with nutmeg and salt. Serve with rice and, if you like, additional sambal ulek.

Variation:
Spinach soup with prawns
(Bobor bayam udang)
Follow the above recipe, adding 250 g peeled, cooked prawns or shrimps with the sweetcorn in Step 2. Rinse the prawns or shrimps under cold running water and pat dry before use.

Corn fritters

Simple • Madura

Perkedel jagung

340 g can sweetcorn
150 g cooked, peeled prawns
2 shallots
1 garlic clove
1 egg
100 g flour
½ tsp sambal ulek (page 42)
1 tsp ground coriander
salt
½ litre oil for deep-frying
1 red chili flower (see Note, right)

Preparation time: 30 minutes

430 kJ/100 calories per fritter

1 Rinse the sweetcorn under running water and drain through a sieve. Rinse the prawns under cold running water, drain and chop coarsely. Peel and finely chop the shallots and garlic.

2 Whisk the egg in a bowl. Sift the flour into the egg. Add the sweetcorn, prawns, shallots and garlic together with the *sambal ulek*, coriander and salt, and knead to a dough.

3 Heat the oil in a saucepan or deep-fryer until very hot. Drop teaspoonsful of the dough into the oil, and deep-fry, in batches, for about 3 minutes until golden and crisp.

4 Transfer the cooked fritters with a slotted spoon onto kitchen paper to drain off the surplus oil. Serve hot or cold as a snack, or as part of a *rijstafel*, garnished with the chili flower.

Note: To make the chili flower garnish, take a large red chili pepper and cut in half lengthwise to almost the stalk. Discard the seeds. Make several more lengthwise cuts until you have 6 or 8 petals. (Don't forget that the chili's volatile oils may irritate the skin, so keep your hands well away from your eyes and wash your hands thoroughly.) Place the chili pepper in ice-cold water for about 30 minutes. The strips will roll up to look like flower petals.

Peanut croquettes

Simple • Party snack

Rempeyek kacang

2 shallots
1 garlic clove
150 g roasted peanuts
¼ litre canned unsweetened coconut milk
½ tsp turmeric
1 tsp ground coriander
1 tsp ground cumin
salt
150 g rice flour (or, if unavailable, wheat flour)
½ litre oil for deep-frying

Preparation time: 30 minutes

300 kJ/71 calories per croquette

1 Peel and finely chop the shallots. Peel and crush the garlic. Coarsely chop the peanuts or, if you prefer, leave them whole; but it is easier to form neat croquettes with chopped peanuts.

2 Put the shallots, garlic and peanuts in a bowl together with the coconut milk, spices, some salt and the flour. Mix well, then knead into a dough.

3 Heat the oil in a saucepan or deep-fryer until very hot. With floured hands, shape the dough into about 20 croquettes the size of a plum, or drop the dough a teaspoonful at a time into the oil, and fry in batches for about 3 minutes until golden.

4 Transfer the fried croquettes with a slotted spoon onto kitchen paper to drain. Serve hot or cold as a snack, or as part of a *rijsttafel*.

Variation:
Coconut croquettes (*Rempeyek teri*) Instead of peanuts, use grated coconut, fresh or from a packet.

Note: The croquettes can be sprinkled with a grated coconut and peanut mixture (*page 71*).

Prawn crackers

Quick and easy • Java **Krupuk**   *Serves 4*

¼ litre oil for deep-frying
100 g small or 4 large ready-to-
cook prawn crackers

Preparation time: 10 minutes

460 kJ/110 calories per portion

1 Heat the oil in a saucepan or deep-fryer. It is hot enough when bubbles rise from a wooden chopstick plunged into the hot oil.

2 Fry the prawn crackers in small batches—they only take a few seconds before they swell to double their size, but there should still be room enough for them to float freely in the oil. When cooked, they should be puffy and crisp. It is essential not to let them go brown, otherwise they will taste bitter. Best of all, fry one crisp as a trial.

3 Remove the cooked crisps from the oil with a slotted spoon, drain on kitchen paper and serve at once.

Note: Prawn crackers are a good accompaniment to practically any Indonesian dish. These crackers, made from ground prawns and tapioca flour, are also a favourite between-meal snack, rather like potato crisps. You can buy ready-to-cook prawn crackers, in various sizes under different names: *krupuk udang*, *kroepoek*, prawn crackers or *beignets de crevettes*. Uncooked, they look shiny and pale. Many Oriental food shops also sell them in different colours.

Cucumber salad

Quick and easy • Sulawesi **Slada ketimun**   *Serves 4*

1 large cucumber
1 bunch thin young spring onions,
or 4 to 5 larger ones
2 to 3 tbsp white vinegar
1 tsp sugar
salt
½ tsp sambal ulek (page 42)
few sprigs watercress (optional)

Preparation time: 10 minutes

160 kJ/38 calories per portion

1 Peel the cucumber, cut it in half lengthwise and remove the seeds. Then cut it into small squares and put them in a bowl. Trim and wash the spring onions, cut them diagonally into thin rings and add them to the cucumber.

2 Put the vinegar, sugar, salt and *sambal ulek* in another bowl and mix well together. Pour the dressing over the cucumber and spring onions and toss thoroughly. If you like, garnish with watercress. Cucumber salad can be served with any meal.

Variation:

Pickled cucumber (*Acar ketimun*) Simmer 10 cl vinegar, 6 tbsp lemon juice, 2 tsp sugar and ½ tsp salt over low heat for about 2 minutes. Add 1 whole chili pepper and 1 sliced onion, and simmer for 1 minute more. Layer diced cucumber in a preserving jar. Top up with the vinegar mixture, and seal the jar so that it is airtight. Shake the jar thoroughly. Pickle cucumber will keep for several weeks.

Tofu with peanut sauce

Fairly easy • Java **Tahu petis** *Serves 4*

2 pieces fresh, or vacuum-packed,
firm tofu (about 250 g each)
¼ litre oil for deep-frying
salt

For the peanut sauce:
2 shallots • 3 garlic cloves
100 g roasted peanuts
pinch of terasi (see page 96)
3 tbsp kecap manis (sweet soy sauce)
juice of ½ lemon
1 tsp sambal ulek (page 42)
2 tsp palm or soft brown sugar
2 tbsp peanut oil
30 cl unsweetened coconut milk
or water

Preparation time: 35 minutes

2,700 kJ/640 calories
per portion

1 Thoroughly drain the tofu. Cut each piece of tofu in half lengthwise, then into strips about 1 cm wide—to make about 40 pieces. Heat the oil in a large frying pan over medium heat. Fry the tofu in batches for about 5 minutes until golden and crisp on both sides. Remove from the pan with a slotted spoon onto kitchen paper to drain.

2 Peel and coarsely chop the shallots. Peel the garlic. Put the shallots and garlic in a food processor or blender with the peanuts, *terasi, kecap manis,* lemon juice, *sambal ulek* and sugar, and blend to a thick paste.

3 Heat the peanut oil in a small frying pan and briefly fry the peanut paste. Pour in the coconut milk or water. Simmer over a low heat for about 2 minutes, stirring constantly.

4 Carefully stir the tofu into the peanut sauce. Season lightly with salt and serve as a salad or as an accompaniment to rice, with grated coconut and peanuts (*page 71*).

Note: Tofu is a nutritious and economical substitute for meat or fish. Cholesterol-free and low in calories, it contains a high level of protein. Fresh tofu preserved in water keeps in the refrigerator for up to a week. Unopened vacuum-packed tofu will keep for many months.

Tofu in soy sauce

Not difficult • Java   **Tahu kecap**   *Serves 4*

2 shallots
5 garlic cloves
4 cm piece fresh ginger
2 pieces fresh, or vacuum-packed, firm tofu (about 250 g each)
¼ litre oil for deep-frying
3 tbsp soy sauce
3 tbsp kecap manis (sweet soy sauce)
3 tbsp tomato ketchup
salt

Preparation time: 30 minutes

520 kJ/120 calories per portion

1 Peel and finely chop the shallots and garlic. Peel and finely grate the ginger.

2 Thoroughly drain the tofu. Cut each piece of tofu in half lengthwise, then into strips about 1 cm wide—to make about 40 pieces. Heat the oil in a large frying pan over medium heat. Fry the tofu in batches for about 5 minutes until golden and crisp on both sides. Remove from the pan with a slotted spoon onto kitchen paper to drain and keep warm.

3 Pour off most of the oil, leaving about 2 tbsp in the pan. Fry the shallots, garlic and ginger over medium heat, until transparent. Add the soy sauce, *kecap manis* and the ketchup,

then add the tofu and stir carefully until heated through. Season with a little salt. Serve with rice and chili-tomato sauce (*page 44*).

Variation:
Sweet-and-sour tofu
(*Tahu asam manis*)
Prepare the tofu as described above. To make the sauce, soak 1 walnut-sized piece of tamarind pulp in 20 cl hot water for 10 minutes and follow the instructions on page 46, Step 1, top recipe. Make the sauce as above (*Steps 1 and 3*), using half the quantities, and stir in 5 tbsp palm sugar and the tamarind juice at the same time as the soy sauces.

Tofu with bean sprouts

Fairly easy • Java **Tumis tahu tauge** *Serves 4*

**2 pieces fresh, or vacuum-packed,
firm tofu (about 250 g each)**
¼ litre oil for deep-frying
200 g bean sprouts
**½ bunch thin young spring onions,
or 2 to 3 larger ones**
½ cucumber • salt
2 to 3 garlic cloves
2 tbsp soy sauce
**4 tbsp kecap manis (sweet
soy sauce)**
½ tsp sambal ulek (page 42)
2 tsp palm or soft brown sugar

Preparation time: 35 minutes

590 kJ/140 calories per portion

1 Thoroughly drain the tofu. Cut each piece of tofu in half lengthwise, then into strips about 1 cm wide, as on pages 116 and 117, or into 3 cm squares, as illustrated opposite. Heat the oil in a large frying pan over medium heat. Fry the tofu in batches for about 5 minutes until golden and crisp on both sides. Remove from the pan with a slotted spoon onto kitchen paper to drain.

2 Pour boiling water over the bean sprouts and drain through a colander. Trim and wash the spring onions and cut them diagonally into thin rings. Peel the cucumber, cut in half lengthwise, remove the seeds, then cut into small cubes. Arrange the tofu, bean sprouts, spring onions and cucumber on a serving dish—or, if you prefer, place the tofu on a separate dish. Sprinkle the vegetables with salt.

3 For the dressing, peel and crush the garlic, put it in a bowl with the soy sauce, *kecap manis* and *sambal ulek* and stir. Dissolve the palm sugar in 1 tbsp hot water and stir into the dressing. Sprinkle over the vegetables. Serve as a salad, or as a side-dish with rice, accompanied by chili-soy sauce (*page 42*) omitting the spring onions.

Soya beans

Soya beans are one of the oldest food crops known to have been cultivated in China and Southeast Asia. This wonder bean is more nutritious and versatile in its uses than practically any other vegetable. Soya bean products are a source of protein for people who cannot afford meat. As a result, soya beans are processed in a variety of ways, from cooking oil to a wide range of concentrated pastes and sauces.

They are also used to make tofu, a complete food, creamy white in colour and neutral in flavour, which is a staple in Indonesia where it is known as *tahu*. Usually sold in cakes, either fresh or vacuum-packed, the protein-rich bean curd is often deep-fried until golden and served in a sauce or with vegetables.

Another traditional Indonesian soya bean product is *tempeh*, made by soaking and peeling the beans, which are then steamed and dried off. Within a few days of being injected with a culture which causes fermentation, they turn into a compact, white cake in which the beans retain their shape, and which contains up to 50 per cent high-grade protein. Not as widely available here as tofu, *tempeh* is sold by Indonesian and other well-stocked Oriental food stores.

Fried soya bean cake

Fairly easy • Java and Bali **Tempeh goreng** **Serves 4**

*1 bunch thin young spring onions,
or 4 to 5 larger ones
3 garlic cloves
450 g tempeh (see Box, page 118)
¼ litre oil for deep-frying
1 tsp sambal ulek (page 42)
2 tsp palm sugar (or, if unavailable,
soft brown sugar)
salt
6 tbsp kecap manis (sweet
soy sauce)*

Preparation time: 30 minutes

480 kJ/110 calories per portion

1 Trim and wash the spring onions, and cut them diagonally into thin rings. Peel and crush the garlic.

2 Cut the *tempeh* in half lengthwise, then cut into slices about 1 cm wide (*above*), making about 30 pieces.

3 Heat the oil in a large frying pan over medium heat. Fry the *tempeh* slices in batches for 2 to 3 minutes until crisp on both sides. Make sure that the slices are cooked through, because only then will they lose their slightly sour, musty flavour. Transfer the cooked slices onto kitchen paper to drain (*above*).

4 When you have fried all the *tempeh*, there should only be a little oil left in the pan (pour some off, if necessary). Fry the spring onions and garlic over a medium heat in the remaining oil, until transparent. Add the *sambal ulek*, sugar, a little salt and the *kecap manis*. Simmer for another minute or so, until the sauce thickens. Return the *tempeh* to the pan and stir carefully into the sauce. Serve hot or cold.

Variations:
Sweet-and-sour tempeh
(*Tempeh asam manis*)
Deep-fry the *tempeh* as described above. To make the sauce, soak 1 walnut-sized piece of tamarind pulp in 20 cl hot water for 10 minutes and follow the instructions on page 46, Step 1, top recipe. Make the sauce as in Steps 1 and 4 above, adding 5 tbsp palm sugar (instead of 2 tsp), 3 tbsp *kecap manis* (instead of 6 tbsp) and the tamarind juice.

Tempeh with bean sprouts
(*Tempeh tumis tauge*)
Deep-fry the *tempeh* as described above. Prepare the sauce according to the recipe for tofu with bean sprouts on page 118.

Note: This vegetarian dish provides high-grade protein and is easy to digest. Like all soya bean products, *tempeh* will readily absorb the flavours of the ingredients with which it is cooked.

DESSERTS

With the extravagant array of tropical fruits grown in Indonesia, it is not surprising that most Indonesian meals end with fresh fruit or a fruit salad.

As well as bananas, pineapples, papayas and mangoes, there are lychees, red rambutans covered in soft hairy spines and yellow five-ribbed carambola, or starfruit. Other exotic fruits include mangosteens, with purplish skins and exquisite sweet-and-sour flavoured white flesh; jackfruit (known locally as *nangka*), an oval green fruit weighing up to 20 kg, sweet and juicy when ripe; and the durian, as big as a water melon, with creamy, custard-like flesh—for many Southeast Asians the "Queen of Fruits" despite its unpleasant smell when opened.

Indonesians also love sweet dishes. Many are based on a blend of glutinous rice, coconut milk and palm sugar, as, for example, the two-coloured rice cake on page 129. They are served less as desserts than as teatime treats, and enjoyed on special occasions. However, this should not deter you from offering some of these delicious sweetmeats as the finale to your menu—European-style, but with a distinctly Oriental flavour—and we have included them in the Suggested Menus section (*pages 138 to 139*).

Tropical fruit salad

Buah buahan

1 large pineapple
1 soft mango
1 firm papaya
2 ripe carambolas (starfruit)
3 bananas
250 g lychees or rambutans (fresh or canned)
juice of 1 lemon

Preparation time: 20 minutes

1,100 kJ/260 calories per portion

1 Cut the pineapple in half lengthwise, slicing through the crest of leaves. Scoop out the central flesh, leaving a shell about 2 cm thick. Discard the hard core, and cut the rest into cubes. Set the two halves aside.

2 Peel the mango and cut the flesh round the stone into small slices.

3 Peel the papaya with a potato peeler, paring the skin lengthwise in strips. Halve the fruit, scoop out the seeds with a spoon and slice the flesh.

4 Cut the carambolas crosswise into thin star shapes. Peel the bananas and cut into slices about 5 mm thick.

5 If using fresh lychees or rambutans, peel and remove the stones. If using canned fruit, drain off the juice.

6 Place all the prepared fruit in a bowl, sprinkle with the lemon juice and mix together. Transfer to the halved pineapple shells and serve.

Note: Tropical fruits are sensitive to cold, so it is better to store them in a cool place than in the refrigerator.

Mangoes

Many people consider the mango the most delicious fruit in the world. Together with pineapples and bananas, mangoes are the most common fruit grown in Indonesia, and during the time of the mango harvest—from the end of March to late May—the Southeast Asians traditionally eat them every day. Mangoes are reputed to embody health and strength. They are also celebrated in legends and verse: it is said that the fragrance of the mango blossom intensifies the longing of those unrequited in love.

Mangoes grow in many parts of the world and vary in size, shape, colour and flavour. They have a smooth, leathery skin and juicy, sweet or slightly tangy, sometimes fibrous, flesh. Some mangoes are not much bigger than apricots, while others weigh as much as a kilo. They can be round, oval, long or kidney-shaped; green, yellow, orange or bright red.

Ripe mangoes are best eaten raw, either on their own or in a fruit salad. They also make delicious ice cream. Unripe mangoes have a somewhat sharper taste; they can be cooked as a vegetable or in a curry, and are the basis for the universally popular mango chutney.

Fragrant blancmange

Buah buah amandel

Not difficult • Java and Bali

Serves 4

**15 g piece agar-agar (about 15 cm)
or ½ packet powdered agar-agar
30 cl milk
150 g sugar
1½ tsp almond extract
400 g fresh pineapple
100 g lychees**

**Preparation time: 35 minutes
(plus 12 to 16 hours' soaking and
chilling time)**

1,100 kJ/260 calories per portion

1 Cut the piece of agar-agar, if using, into 2 cm pieces and soak overnight in cold water.

2 Next day, put the milk and sugar in a shallow pan with 30 cl water and bring to the boil. Squeeze the moisture from the agar-agar, add the pieces to the pan, return to the boil, then reduce the heat to low and simmer for about 5 minutes, stirring constantly. If you are using powdered agar-agar, stir it into the same amount of water, milk and sugar, and simmer over low heat for about 5 minutes, stirring constantly.

3 Remove from the heat, and leave to cool for about 20 minutes. Stir in the almond extract. Rinse out 4 individual

moulds, or a jelly mould, with cold water and pour in the mixture. Cover and refrigerate for at least 4 hours.

4 Cut the pineapple into cubes. Peel the lychees. Turn the blancmange out onto a dish and serve with the pineapple and lychees.

Note: Canned lychees and pineapple chunks can be substituted for the fresh fruit. Agar-agar, produced from seaweed, is a more powerful gelling agent than gelatine. Available in sheet or powder form, you will find it in Oriental or health food stores, sometimes under the Japanese name *kanten*. Powdered agar-agar is now available in a variety of colours.

Steamed coconut pudding

Serikaya

Simple • Sumatra and Java

Serves 4

**1 tbsp butter or margarine
3 eggs
100 g palm sugar (or, if unavailable,
soft brown sugar)
40 cl canned unsweetened coconut
milk
pinch of salt
50 g fresh or dried coconut flakes**

**Preparation time: 40 minutes
(plus 6 hours' chilling time)**

870 kJ/210 calories per portion

1 Grease an ovenproof pudding basin with the butter or margarine.

2 In a bowl, whisk the eggs with 90 g of the sugar until frothy, then stir in the coconut milk and a pinch of salt. Pour the mixture into the basin.

3 Stand the pudding basin in a saucepan. Pour enough hot water into the pan to reach two thirds of the way up the side of the basin. Bring the water to the boil, reduce the heat to low, cover the pan and steam the

pudding for at least 30 minutes, until set. Top the pan up with water, if necessary. Remove the pudding from the pan and leave in a cool place for at least 6 hours.

4 Heat a frying pan without fat over low heat and dry fry the coconut flakes for about 5 minutes, stirring constantly, until golden-brown. Mix with the rest of the sugar and place in a dessert bowl. Turn out the cold pudding, cut it into wedges and arrange them on the toasted coconut.

Two-coloured rice cake

More complex • Sumatra **Kue putuh mayang** *Makes 8 to 12 portions*

250 g glutinous rice
40 cl canned unsweetened coconut milk
1 tbsp butter or margarine
2 daun pandan (screw pine) leaves
3 eggs
90 g palm sugar (or, if unavailable, soft brown sugar)
30 g tapioca flour
4 drops daun pandan essence (green food colouring)
2 drops vanilla extract

Preparation time: 1½ hours (plus 5 hours' soaking and cooling time)

530 kJ/130 calories per portion (if serving 12)

1 Rinse the rice until the water runs clear, drain, then place in a bowl with enough cold water to cover. Leave to stand for at least 2 hours, then drain. Steam the rice for 10 minutes, covered, in a lined sieve over a pan of boiling water—or cook it in a rice steamer—then remove from the heat.

2 Heat a large non-stick frying pan. Mix the rice with 15 cl of the coconut milk, pour into the pan and stir over low heat for about 2 minutes (*above*), until the rice has absorbed all the coconut milk. Remove the pan from the heat. Reheat the steamer. Return the rice to the steamer, cover and continue to steam for about another 15 minutes, until the rice is tender.

3 Grease a 24 cm cake tin with the butter or margarine. Transfer the rice to the tin, and press down into a firm, even layer.

4 Fold the *daun pandan* leaves and place them in a cup. Pour on 3 cl (about 3 tbsp) boiling water (*above*), and leave to cool. Meanwhile, whisk the eggs with the sugar, then fold in the tapioca flour.

5 Remove the leaves from the water which will have taken on their flavour. Stir the water into the egg mixture, together with the rest of the coconut milk, the *daun pandan* essence and vanilla extract.

6 Spread the egg mixture evenly on top of the rice in the cake tin. Stand the tin in a saucepan, add enough hot water to the pan to come two thirds up the side of the tin and bring to the boil. Reduce the heat to low and steam, covered, for about 1 hour, until the egg mixture is set. Using a knife, carefully loosen the cake round the edge. Leave to cool for at least 3 hours, then turn out onto a serving dish and cut into slices.

Glutinous rice dumplings

Onde onde

Serves 4

250 g glutinous rice flour
salt
3 drops daun pandan (screw pine)
essence (green food colouring)
70 g palm sugar in lumps
100 g grated fresh or desiccated
coconut

Preparation time: 1¼ hours

1,700 kJ/400 calories per portion

1 Place the glutinous rice flour in a mixing bowl with a pinch of salt. Stir the green food colouring into ¼ litre water. A tablespoonful at a time, add the green water to the flour and work the mixture into a dough. Transfer the dough to an unfloured work surface and continue to knead until smooth. It should not stick to your fingers and should be malleable without crumbling.

2 In a large pan, bring 2 litres lightly salted water to the boil. Meanwhile, cut the palm sugar into 7 mm cubes.

3 Break off one third of the dough and shape it into 12 to 15 little dumplings. Hollow out the middle of each dumpling with your index finger and place a cube of palm sugar in each. Firmly reseal the opening. Place the dumplings in the boiling water, turn the heat down low, and simmer for about 15 minutes, turning several times.

4 The dumplings are ready when they float to the surface. Carefully remove them from the water with a slotted spoon and drain through a sieve.

5 Cook the remaining two batches in the same way as the first, preparing the second batch while the first is cooking. Never work all the dough at once, otherwise it will become too crumbly and sugar will flow out while cooking. If the dough becomes too dry, knead it again thoroughly with wet hands.

6 Coat the cooked dumplings in the coconut and arrange on a serving dish.

Sweet potato in coconut milk

Kolak ubi

Serves 6

500 g sweet potatoes
½ litre canned unsweetened
coconut milk
100 g palm sugar (or, if unavailable,
soft brown sugar)
salt

Preparation time: 30 minutes

560 kJ/130 calories per portion

1 Carefully peel and wash the sweet potatoes, then cut them into cubes.

2 Slowly heat the coconut milk, and dissolve the sugar in it. Add the sweet potato cubes and a pinch of salt. Cover the pan and cook over a low heat for about 20 minutes until tender. Serve hot or cold.

Note: Sweet potatoes have a very high starch content. They can be white, red or yellow; the yellow ones taste best. They are prepared in the same way as potatoes, but with a little less salt.

Coconut pancake rolls

Fairly easy • Sumatra **Dadar gulung** *Makes 6 rolls*

For the filling:
5 tbsp palm sugar (or, if unavailable, soft brown sugar)
100 g grated fresh or desiccated coconut

For the batter:
20 cl unsweetened coconut milk
6 drops green or other food colouring
2 eggs • 150 g flour
salt • 3 tbsp oil

Preparation time: 45 minutes

800 kJ/190 calories per roll

1 To make the filling, place the palm sugar in a saucepan with 10 cl water. Heat through, stirring constantly until the sugar has completely dissolved. Add 80 g of the coconut and simmer over a low heat, stirring constantly until the coconut has absorbed all the liquid. Remove the pan from the heat and leave to cool.

2 Meanwhile, prepare the pancakes. Put the coconut milk into a bowl and stir in the food colouring. Break the eggs into another bowl and whisk until frothy, then add them to the coconut milk. Gradually stir in the sifted flour and a pinch of salt.

3 Grease a frying pan with 1 tsp oil. Heat the pan and add a ladleful of batter. The pancake should be as thin as possible. Fry until the underside is golden-brown, then turn and briefly cook the other side, and remove from the pan. After each pancake is cooked, add 1 tsp oil to the pan for the next one. Keep the pancakes warm until they are all cooked.

4 To stuff the pancakes, place 1 tbsp of the coconut filling at the lower edge of each pancake. Fold the sides inwards and roll up from the filling end. Serve on a warmed dish, sprinkled with the remaining coconut.

Peanut-sesame pancakes

Takes a little time • Sumbawa

Kue apem

Makes 6 to 8 pancakes

70 g unsalted peanuts
3 tbsp sesame seeds
5 tbsp sugar
2 eggs
250 g flour
3 tsp baking powder
salt
2 tbsp peanut oil
¼ litre milk
4 tbsp oil for frying

Preparation time: 1 hour

1,300 kJ/310 calories per pancake
(if serving 8)

1 Coarsely grind the peanuts and put them in a dry frying pan with the sesame seeds over low heat. Dry fry them for about 2 minutes, stirring constantly. Transfer to a bowl, mix with 4 tbsp of the sugar, then set aside.

2 Whisk the eggs and 1 tbsp sugar in a bowl until frothy. Sift in the flour, then add the baking powder, salt, peanut oil and milk, and stir thoroughly. Gradually add 12.5 cl water and mix to make a thin batter.

3 Heat 1 tsp oil in a medium-sized frying pan over medium heat. Pour in a ladleful of batter at a time over a medium heat. When the pancake has set and begins to brown, sprinkle with 2 tbsp of the peanut and sesame mixture, cover the pan and continue to cook for a further 2 to 3 minutes. Remove from the pan, fold in half and keep warm. Repeat the process with the rest of the batter, adding 1 tsp oil to the pan after cooking each pancake. Arrange on a serving dish and serve.

Cassava cake

Bingka singkong

1.5 kg fresh or frozen cassava roots
(or, if unavailable, dried cassava)
2 tbsp margarine or butter
2 eggs
salt
300 g sugar
½ litre canned unsweetened
coconut milk

Preparation time: 1¼ hours
(plus 1½ hours' cooling time)

930 kJ/220 calories per portion
(if serving 8)

1 Peel the cassava roots, remove and discard the fibrous outer layer of white flesh. Finely grate the flesh, then, a batch at a time, squeeze out as much moisture as possible. If you are using defrosted cassava roots, grate finely.

2 Preheat the oven to 220°C (425°F or Mark 7). Grease a shallow 25 by 30 cm baking dish with the butter or margarine. Whisk the eggs in a bowl with a pinch of salt until frothy, then add the sugar. Add the coconut milk and grated cassava to the eggs and stir thoroughly. In a non-stick frying pan over medium heat, cook the mixture for about 5 minutes, stirring constantly, until it becomes sticky and transparent.

3 Transfer the cassava mixture to the baking dish, smooth the surface and bake in the centre of the oven for about 45 minutes until golden-brown on top. Remove from the oven and leave to cool before cutting into pieces.

Note: Cassava, or manioc, is cultivated in Indonesia mainly in the eastern islands. The roots, up to 50 cm long and 5 to 10 cm thick, have a high starch content and are commercially processed into tapioca. The sap of raw bitter cassava is poisonous and the roots should always be cooked.

Banana balls

Jumput pisang goreng

2 very ripe bananas
3 tbsp brown sugar
100 g flour
½ litre oil for deep-frying
2 tbsp grated fresh or desiccated
coconut (optional)

Preparation time: 15 minutes

180 kJ/31 calories per ball

1 Purée the bananas with a fork or in a blender, then stir in the sugar and flour to make a dough.

2 Heat the oil in a saucepan or deep-fryer until small bubbles rise up from a wooden chopstick or wooden spoon handle dipped into the oil.

3 Put a teaspoonful at a time of the banana dough in the hot oil and deep-fry for about 2 minutes until golden. Remove from the pan and drain on kitchen paper. If you like, sprinkle with grated coconut, and serve hot.

Note: Bananas are among the world's most nutritious fruits. They are rich in vitamins A, B_1, B_2. B_6, C and E, and niacin. They also contain lots of minerals, including potassium, phosphorus, iron and magnesium, as well as dietary fibre. (*See also page 136.*)

Banana fritters

Pisang goreng

Serves 4

1 egg
1 tbsp palm or soft brown sugar
4 tbsp cornflour
2 tbsp tapioca flour
½ tsp baking powder
¼ tsp salt
2 tbsp fresh grated or desiccated coconut
50 cl canned unsweetened coconut milk
4 bananas (preferably not ripe)
½ litre oil for deep-frying

Preparation time: 20 minutes

830 kJ/200 calories per portion

1 To make the batter, whisk the egg and sugar in a bowl. Stir in the cornflour, tapioca flour, baking powder, salt, coconut and coconut milk, and mix thoroughly. Leave to stand for about 10 minutes.

2 Meanwhile, peel the bananas and cut them in half lengthwise.

3 Heat the oil in a deep frying pan or deep-fryer over medium heat, until small bubbles rise from a wooden chopstick or wooden spoon handle dipped into the oil.

4 Dip the banana halves a few at a time in the batter to coat them, then deep-fry them in the hot oil for about 4 minutes, turning once. Remove from the pan and drain on kitchen paper. Serve hot.

Variation:
Pineapple fritters (*Nanas goreng*) Use pineapple slices instead of bananas. Other fruits can also be fried in batter, as can tofu.

Bananas

Bananas are one of the world's most ancient cultivated plants. N. W. Simmonds, in his book *Bananas,* says that they were probably grown for food tens of thousands of years ago in Southeast Asia.

The banana plant is a tree-like herbaceous giant belonging to the *Musa* family that in only one year grows to a height of up to 10 metres. It bears just one multiple fruit, but this can weigh up to 50 kg and consists of about 200 bananas. When immature, these grow hanging downwards, but soon make a full turn and proceed to grow with their tips pointing towards the source of light—hence their curved shape.

There are many different varieties of banana, with wide variations in size and flavour. In Southeast Asia, the favourite table variety is the sugar or baby banana. It is quite tiny, only 10 to 12 cm long, but its sweetness and fragrance is unsurpassed. An unusual speciality is the red banana.

As well as eating bananas raw, Indonesians fry them in batter or grill them to serve with meat. The banana leaves are used to wrap food for steaming or baking.

A close relative, the plantain, is hard and green and contains more starch. Used like potatoes, plantains can be boiled, steamed, fried, puréed or deep-fried in oil.

Suggested Menus

The following menus, based on recipes in this book, are only a general guide to help you to plan for different occasions. For a *rijsttafel*, place a large bowl of yellow rice in the centre of the table, with the other dishes crowded round it. Each guest is provided with a rice bowl or plate and a spoon and fork. Fruit and desserts are served at the end of the meal.

Family menus

Special fried rice with vegetables	32
Prawn crackers	115
Cucumber salad	115
Fried chicken Javanese-style (*variation*)	83
Coconut rice	31
Fish in soy sauce	89
Curried noodles with tofu (*variation*)	59
Sweet potato in coconut milk	130
Chicken soup	80
Rice in banana leaves	38
Vegetables with peanut sauce	98
Fish paté	92
Beef or chicken satay	66
Stuffed rice rolls	37
Curried noodles	59
Peanut-sesame pancakes	133
Stuffed pancakes	104
Steamed rice	28
Lamb curry (*variation*)	55
Spicy fruit salad	96

Regional menus

Balinese-style:
Yellow rice	28
Loin of suckling pig	74
Fried soya bean cake	120
Coconut croquettes (*variation*)	112
Banana fritters	136

Sumatra-style:
Steamed rice	28
Spiced beef in coconut milk	55
Calf's liver curry	56
Fried prawn sambal	51
Aubergine sambal	51
Spinach soup	110
Steamed coconut pudding	126

Javanese-style:
Spinach soup with prawns (*variation*)	110
Coconut rice	31
Tofu with bean sprouts	118
Sweet chili-soy sauce (*variation*)	42
Steamed coconut pudding	126

Steamed rice	28
Meatballs with coconut milk (*variation*)	68
Stir-fried vegetables	102
Pineapple fritters (*variation*)	136

National specialities

Chicken soup	80
Fried rice	34
Prawn crackers	115
Cucumber salad	115
Beef or chicken satay	66
Stuffed rice rolls	37
Banana fritters	136
Vegetables with peanut sauce	98
Steamed rice	28
Lamb curry (*variation*)	55
Chili-tomato sauce	44
Fried flatbread (*variation*)	105
Coconut pancake rolls	132

Meat-based menus

Chicken soup	80
Indonesian spring rolls	107
Coconut rice	31
Sweet-and-sour pork	76
Ripe jackfruit (canned)	—
Beef soup	72
Rice in banana leaves	38
Spiced beef in coconut milk	55
Fried flatbread (*variation*)	105
Spicy fruit salad	96
Stuffed rice rolls	37
Sweet chili-soy sauce (*variation*)	42
Chili-tomato sauce	44
Yellow rice	28
Beef sambal	46
Fresh tropical fruit (for example, mangoes, papayas, lychees, rambutan or pineapple)	—

Fish-based menus

Spinach soup with prawns (*variation*)	110
Coconut rice	31
Fried squid sambal	48
Baked spiced mackerel	89
Fragrant blancmange, served with fresh mango slices	126
Sour vegetable soup (enriched with 400 g cooked squid)	108
Steamed rice	28
Fried prawn sambal	51
Fish curry	60
Vegetable salad with coconut	100
Fresh pineapple*	—

Vegetables in coconut milk (enriched with 100 g cooked prawns)	110
Sweet-and-sour fish	90
Prawn crackers	115
Banana fritters	136
Pineapple fritters (*variation*)	136

Meatless menus

Steamed rice	28
Aubergine curry	63
Vegetables in coconut milk	110
Tofu in soy sauce	117
Cucumber salad	115
Vegetables with peanut sauce	98
Rice in banana leaves	38
Fried soya bean cake	120
Sour vegetable soup	108
Fresh fruit	—
Steamed rice	28
Eggs in chili sauce	45
Peanut croquettes	112
Cucumber salad	115
Two-coloured rice cake	129

Quick menus

Steamed rice	28
Javanese meatballs	71
Chili-tomato sauce	44
Sour vegetable soup	108
Coconut pancake rolls	132
Steamed rice	28
Jackfruit curry	54
Pickled cucumber (*variation*)	115
Pork fillet in soy sauce	76
Tropical fruit salad	124

Inexpensive menus

Stuffed pancakes	104
Fried noodles (*variation*)	33
Poached eggs*	—
Prawn crackers	115
Peanut-sesame pancakes	133
Steamed rice	28
Mixed vegetable curry	62
Spicy fruit salad	96
Banana fritters	136
Yellow rice	28
Vegetables with peanut sauce	98
Fried chicken Balinese-style (*variation*)	83
Banana balls	135

Cold buffet

Yellow coconut rice (*variation*)	28
Beef or chicken satay (sauce served separately)	66
Sea bass baked in banana leaf	91
Meatballs with coconut	68
Cauliflower with chilies	52
Spicy chili sauce (*variation*)	42
Indonesian spring rolls	107
Corn fritters	112
Stuffed rice rolls	37
Coconut pancake rolls (varied colours)	132
Tropical fruit salad	124
Two-coloured rice cake	129

Rijsttafel for 6 to 8

Yellow rice	28
Chili-soy sauce	42
Chili-tomato sauce	44
Prawn crackers	115
Stir-fried vegetables	102
Chicken soup	80
Meatballs with coconut milk (*variation*)	68
Sweet-and-sour pork	76
Spiced beef in coconut milk	55
Fish in soy sauce	89
Spiced prawn balls	92
Tropical fruit salad	124
Fragrant blancmange	126
Later in the evening: Glutinous rice dumplings	130

Rijsttafel for 15 to 20

To the suggested dishes above, add 10 to 12 dishes from the following, making sure there is plenty of rice. Sambals and curries can be prepared up to 2 days in advance and refrigerated, then reheated.

Corn fritters	112
Peanut croquettes	112
Fish paté	92
Javanese meatballs	71
Indonesian spring rolls	107
Green bean sambal	52
Aubergine curry	63
Vegetables in coconut milk	110
Tofu in soy sauce	117
Cucumber salad	115
Spinach soup with prawns (*variation*)	110
Fried chicken	82
Beef or chicken satay	66
Beef sambal	46
Fried fish in batter	86
Baked spiced mackerel	89
Sweet-and-sour prawns (*variation*)	90
Banana fritters	136
Fresh fruit	—

Glossary

This glossary is intended as a brief guide to some less familiar cookery terms and ingredients, including words and items found on Indonesian menus. Ingredients can be found in most Asian and Oriental food shops and larger supermarkets; but spellings and names may vary.

Agar-agar: gelling agent processed from seaweed, available in sheets or powder form, used as a vegetarian alternative to gelatine.

Al dente: literally "to the tooth"; ideal consistency for cooked noodles, vegetables and rice, tender but still firm to the bite.

Bamboo shoots: the shoots of tropical bamboo. Sold canned, the best-quality shoots are known as winter bamboo; ordinary bamboo is less tender.They should be drained thoroughly before use.

Banana leaves: the large, glossy, dark green leaves of the banana tree. Up to 3 metres long, they are used to line serving dishes or to wrap rice and other food for steaming, baking or charcoal grilling. Not themselves edible, they give a delicate flavour to other foods.

Bananas: the tropical fruit of the banana tree. Many varieties of banana grow in Indonesia, used in both sweet and savoury dishes. *See also page 136.*

Bean sprouts: the young sprouts of mung or other beans, used in salads and stir-fried dishes. Rich in vitamins, protein and iron, they are readily available fresh, or can be grown from untreated bean seeds.

Carambola (also called starfruit): the pale golden-yellow fruit of a tree that grows wild in Indonesia. Carambolas are up to 12 cm long, with five sharp-edged ribs, and have a sweet-sour flavour; they can be eaten raw or cooked.

Cardamom: the seed pods of a perennial shrub, related to ginger, used as a spice throughout southern Asia and the Middle East. The pods, which contain highly aromatic seeds, can be bought whole or ground. Green cardamom pods have a better flavour than the brown variety.

Cassava (also called manioc): the thick starchy roots of two tropical plants of the spurge family, *Manihot esculenta* (bitter cassava) and *M. dulcis* (sweet cassava). Bitter cassava is grown extensively in Indonesia and Malaysia. It is the source of arrowroot and tapioca and used mainly as a thickening agent. Because its sap contains hydrocyanic acid the root is poisonous when raw and should only be eaten when cooked. Dried cassava can be used grated in cakes and other dishes. Sweet cassava is not poisonous, can be eaten raw and is cooked as a vegetable.

Cellophane noodles (also called bean thread noodles): noodles made from mung bean or other vegetable starch. They are available in varying round or flat thicknesses and when soaked in hot water become soft and slippery.

Chili pepper: hot red or green peppers of the capsicum family, ranging from the very hot bird's eye chili to milder varieties such as the jalalpeño. Because of the many varieties of chili peppers grown in the tropics, it is difficult to give exact quantities for use in specific recipes. In Indonesia, the best-known are red chili peppers (*lombok merah*), used for making *sambal ulek*, green chili peppers (*lombok idijo*) and the fiendishly-hot bird's eye peppers (*lombok rawit*). The seeds of the chili are its hottest part; this should be taken into account when using either fresh or dried chili peppers.
CAUTION: Chilies contain volatile oils that can irritate the skin and cause eyes to burn, so handle them with care and always wash your hands immediately after preparing them.

Chinese cabbage (also called Chinese leaves): an elongated type of cabbage, used in Chinese and Southeast Asian cuisine. It has a subtler taste than European cabbages and is used in salads as well as cooked dishes.

Chinese egg noodles: wheat noodles made with eggs, ranging in size from thick ribbon to vermicelli. They take less time to cook than their Italian equivalent. Readily available, including the popular twisted "nests" of thin noodles.

Coconut: The nut of the coconut palm and a major ingredient in Indonesian cuisine. Coconuts can be bought whole, or ready prepared in flakes, desiccated or grated, and in compressed blocks of creamed coconut. *See also page 31.*

Coconut milk (*santen*): liquid made from grated coconut flesh and water—not the fresh liquid found inside the coconut. It is an essential ingredient in Indonesian cuisine and used to replace not only milk, but butter and other types of fat. Coconut milk can be made from the fresh flesh, but is available in cans or in compressed blocks of creamed coconut. When buying in cans, make sure it is unsweetened coconut milk—though sweetened milk can be used for desserts—and stir before use.

To reconstitute creamed coconut, use approximately 20 cl hot water for every 6 tbsp coconut. To make your own coconut milk, blend the grated flesh of a fresh coconut with 50 cl very hot water in a food processor. Strain through a muslin-lined sieve into a bowl, squeezing out as much fluid as possible. To obtain more, but thinner, milk repeat the process with the coconut dregs and more water. Fresh coconut milk does not keep long, but can be frozen.

Coconut oil: A white oil produced from the dried kernel of the coconut. It has a nutty taste and is suitable for deep and shallow frying.

Coriander: the leaves and seeds of the coriander plant, both common seasonings in Mediterranean, Indian and Southeast Asian cooking. Indonesians use fresh coriander leaves as garnish in the same way as Europeans use parsley. The ground seeds are added to curries and other dishes.

Cumin: the seed of the cumin plant, resembling caraway seeds but with a sweetish, mildly bitter and peppery taste. Available whole and ground.

Curry leaves: highly aromatic leaves, similar to the European bay leaves. Sold fresh on the stem or dried, they are called *daun salaam* in Indonesia and are used to flavour rice, curries and other dishes. Bay leaves make a good substitute.

Daun pandan (screw pine): young leaves of the screw pine tree, used to add flavour and colour to pastries and desserts. They are not always easy to come by. If they are not sold as either *daun pandan* or screw pine leaves, try asking for them by their Thai name: *bai doi. Daun pandan* is also available in essence form, often sold under the Thai name, *bai tuey*.

Daun salaam: *see* Curry leaves.

Durian: melon-sized fruit with a spiky skin. Though it has an unpleasant pungent smell when opened, the Southeast Asians consider its creamy custard-like flesh to be delicious.

Galangal (also called Thai ginger): a rhizome similar to ginger but with a more delicate, slightly sweetish taste. Galangal should be fresh and plump and used as soon as possible; it can also be frozen. Young ginger can be used instead, though the taste will not be the same. Galangal is also available dried or in powder form, often called *laos* powder.

Ginger: the spicy, underground stem of the ginger plant, an important ingredient in Asian cuisine. Fresh ginger should be hard and wrinkle free. To store, put the ginger in an unwaxed paper bag, place inside a plastic bag and keep in the refrigerator. Powdered ginger tastes very different and is not a suitable substitute.

Glutinous rice: round-grained starchy rice used mainly for sweet dishes in Southeast Asia but in some areas it replaces steamed long-grain rice as an accompaniment to savoury dishes. Indonesians often serve steamed glutinous rice wrapped in banana leaves.

Jackfruit (*nangka*): tropical fruit related to the breadfruit. Pumpkin-shaped, with pale mauve flesh, a jackfruit can weigh up to 20 kg. When ripe it is sweet and juicy and can be eaten raw, but it is more often used unripe and cooked in curries and other dishes. Also available canned.

Kecap asin: salty Indonesian soy sauce. *See also page 34.*

Kecap manis: sweet Indonesian soy sauce. *See also page 34.*

Kemiri nuts: the nuts of an Indonesian tree that grows especially in the Moluccas and is used, grated, to thicken curries and soups as well as to flavour meat and fish dishes. *See also page 109.*

Krupuk (prawn crackers): Indonesian speciality, larger than other prawn crackers, most commonly made from finely ground prawns and tapioca flour, cut into thin slices and dried in the sun. When deep-fried in oil they become puffy and crisp and are served as a snack or garnish to cooked dishes. Both *krupuks* and smaller prawn crackers are sold ready-to-cook. *See page 115.*

Lemon grass: thick, fibrous stalks with a lemon flavour, used to flavour soups, pastes and stuffings. *See also page 58.*

Lychee (also spelt litchi): sweetly fragrant round or oval fruit, native to China and Southeast Asia. The succulent white flesh with its single shiny brown seed is encased in a brittle red outer shell. Available fresh and in cans.

Macadamia nuts (also called Queensland nuts): nuts similar in appearance to large hazelnuts, with very hard shells and whitish crisp kernels. Native to Australia, they are also grown in Hawaii and elsewhere. The grated nuts are eaten raw or used in cakes and pastries, and can be substituted for the Indonesian *kemiri* nut. Because the shell is very difficult to crack, macadamia nuts are best bought already shelled. *See also page 109.*

Mango: tropical fruit with a delicious, rich and sticky pulp and a large seed. Eaten ripe as a dessert or cooked unripe as a vegetable. *See also page 125.*

Marinade: a seasoning mixture to coat or soak meat or fish before cooking in order to tenderize or impart flavour.

Palm sugar (*gula jawa*): yellowish-brown sugar made from the sap of the palmyra and other palm trees. Less sweet than white sugar, with a slight caramel flavour, it can be bought in cans or blocks from Oriental and Asian food stores. Demerara or other soft brown sugar can be used instead, but the flavour will be different.

Papaya (also called pawpaw): long, pear-shaped tropical fruit with fragrant, peachy-coloured flesh, reminiscent of melon, and numerous black seeds. Papayas are rich in vitamins A and C, and calcium. A ripe papaya will keep for about a week in a cool, humid place.

Peanuts (also called groundnuts): not nuts but the fruit of a leguminous plant, related to peas and beans, which grows underground. A popular ingredient in Indonesian cookery, especially as a sauce for satay. *See also page 66.*

Prawn crackers: see Krupuk; page 115.

Rambutan: small tropical fruit with a reddish skin covered in soft hairy spines. Its flesh and taste is similar to lychee. Available fresh or canned.

Rice flour: very finely ground flour made from non-glutinous rice (also called rice powder) is used as a thickening agent. Glutinous rice flour is made from ground glutinous rice and used for puddings and to give pastry a sticky consistency.

Sambal ulek: classic Indonesian hot chili sauce, either home-made or sold in jars. *See also page 42.*

Sesame seeds: tiny black or white seeds from the sesame plant used in sweet and savoury dishes, breads and pastries, as well as for making oil.

Shrimp paste: See Terasi.

Soy sauce: savoury seasoning made from fermented soya beans, salt, wheat and yeast. Available in dark and light types. In Indonesia, there are two kinds: thin and salty (*kecap asin*) and thick and sweet (*kecap manis*). *See also page 34.*

Spring onions: type of onion. Indonesian spring onions grow in clumps and are smaller than European ones. They have a delicate, aromatic and mild flavour and are used for seasoning as well as garnish, and as an ingredient in vegetable dishes.

Steaming: to cook food in vapour from boiling water; one of the best techniques for preserving nutrients and flavours.

Stir-fry: Oriental cooking technique in which meat and vegetables are constantly stirred in a wok or frying pan, making them crisp but tender.

Sweet potato (*ubi jalar*): the edible root of *Ipomoea batatas*, grown in tropical countries and brought to Indonesia from Malaysia. They have a very high starch content and are regarded as one of the vegetables most vital to world economy.

Tamarind (*asam*): the pods of the tropical evergreen tamarind tree. The brittle-shelled pods contain a soft, nutty brown pulp, made up of 3 per cent sugar and over 20 per cent fruit acid, from which a sour tangy juice is obtained and used to flavour many Southeast Asian dishes. Tamarind is available in fresh compressed blocks of pulp, which can be soaked in hot water, then kneaded to squeeze out the juice. It is also sold as a concentrated paste in jars.

Tapioca flour: starchy flour produced from the cassava, or manioc, root and used as a thickening agent.

Tempeh: Indonesian soya bean cake, similar to tofu, in which the beans are fermented and left whole. *See also page 118.*

Tofu (also called bean curd): a dense, mild soya bean product. Available in a soft, junket-like variety used in soups, or in firm cakes used for stir-frying, braising or poaching. Its rather bland flavour readily absorbs the flavours of other ingredients. Rich in protein, it is a good vegetarian alternative to meat or fish. Available fresh or vacuum-packed, tofu keeps refrigerated in water for up to 5 days. Drain well before using. *See also page 118.*

Terasi: a protein-rich flavouring made from finely ground, salted, dried shrimps and other seafood and added to many Indonesian dishes. Available in jars or in a dried compressed block, it has a powerful flavour and smell, not to everyone's taste, and should be used in very small amounts. *See also page 96.*

Turmeric: the rhizome of a plant related to ginger, though with a very different smell and flavour. The yellow flesh of the large, fragrant root is ground to produce a yellow powder used as a spice in curries and pickles, and to colour rice yellow in the same way as saffron. Turmeric is also good for the digestion.

Wok: classic Chinese cooking pan that, because of its rounded shape, ensures even heat when stir-frying. A heavy frying pan is a suitable alternative, but tossing food over high heat is easier in a wok because of its depth.

CONVERSION CHART

These figures are not exact equivalents, but have been rounded up or down slightly to make measuring easier.

Weight Equivalents		Volume Equivalents	
Metric	Imperial	Metric	Imperial
15 g	½ oz	8 cl	3 fl oz
30 g	1 oz	12.5 cl	4 fl oz
60 g	2 oz	15 cl	¼ pint
90 g	3 oz	17.5 cl	6 fl oz
125 g	¼ lb	25 cl	8 fl oz
150 g	5 oz	30 cl	½ pint
200 g	7 oz	35 cl	12 fl oz
250 g	½ lb	45 cl	¾ pint
350 g	¾ lb	50 cl	16 fl oz
500 g	1 lb	60 cl	1 pint
1 kg	2 to 2¼ lb	1 litre	35 fl oz

Recipe Index

Aubergine:
  curry 63
  sambal 51

Banana(s): 136
  balls 135
  fritters 136
  leaf, sea bass baked in, 91
  leaves, rice in, 38
  toasted, 74
Barbecued spare ribs 79
Bean sprouts:
  tempeh with (variation), 120
  tofu with, 118
Beef:
  Balinese spiced, 68
  satay 66
  sambal 46
  soup 72
  in soy sauce 71
  spiced, in coconut milk 55
Blancmange, fragrant, 126

Cabbage omelette, fried, 102
Calf's liver curry 56
Cassava cake 135
Cauliflower with chilies 52
Chicken:
  crispy roast, 79
  curry 56
  fried, 82:
    Balinese-style (variation) 83
    Javanese-style (variation) 83
    Sumatra-style (variation) 83
  liver sambal 46
  rice with crispy, 39
  satay 66
  soup 80
Chilies, cauliflower with, 52
Chili sauce (*sambal ulek*): 42
  eggs in, 45
  spicy (variation), 42
Chili-soy sauce 42
Chili-tomato sauce 44
Coconut: 31
  croquettes 112
  grated, with peanuts 71
  meatballs with, 68
  pancake rolls 132
  pudding, steamed, 126
  rice 31;
    yellow (variation), 28
  sauce, red mullet in, 86
  vegetable salad with, 100
Coconut milk:
  meatballs with (variation), 68

spiced beef in, 55
sweet potato in, 130
vegetables in, 110
Corn fritters 112
Croquettes:
coconut (variation), 112
peanut, 112
Cucumber:
pickled (variation), 115
salad 115
Cuttlefish 48

Duck, Bali, 85

Eggs in chili sauce 45

Fish:
curry 60
fried, in batter 86
paté, 92
in soy sauce 89
Flatbread, fried (variation), 105
Fritters:
banana, 136
corn, 112
pineapple (variation), 136
Fruit salad:
spicy, 96
tropical, 124

Green bean sambal 52

Indonesian spring rolls 107

Jackfruit curry 54
Javanese meatballs 71

Kecap manis (sweet soy sauce) 34
Kemiri nuts 109

Lamb:
curry (variation) 55
fried (variation), 46
in soy sauce (variation) 76
Lamb's liver curry (variation) 56

Mackerel, baked spiced, 89
Mangoes 125
Meatballs:
with coconut 68
with coconut milk (variation) 68
Javanese, 71
noodle soup with, 73
Mutton soup (variation) 72

Noodle soup with meatballs 73

Noodles:
curried, 59;
with tofu (variation) 59
fried (variation), 33

Octopus 48
Omelette:
fried cabbage, 102
shredded, 33
Onion rings, crispy fried, 28

Pancake rolls, coconut, 132
Pancakes:
peanut-sesame, 133
stuffed, 104
Paté, fish, 92
Peanut:
croquettes 112
sauce, tofu with, 116
sauce, vegetables with, 98
Peanuts: 66
grated coconut with, 71
Peanut-sesame pancakes 133
Pickled cucumber (variation) 115
Pig, loin of suckling, 74
Pineapple fritters (variation) 136
Pork:
fillet in soy sauce 76
sweet-and-sour, 76
Prawn(s):
balls, spiced, 92
crackers 115
fried, in batter (variation) 86
sambal, fried, 51
sweet-and-sour, sambal
(variation), 51
sweet-and-sour (variation), 90

Red mullet in coconut sauce 86
Rice:
in banana leaves 38
cake, two-coloured, 129
coconut, 31
with crispy chicken 39
dumplings, glutinous, 130
fried, 34
rolls, stuffed, 37
steamed, 28
special fried, 32
stuffed, rolls 37
yellow, 28
yellow coconut (variation), 28

Sambal ulek (chili sauce) 42
Satay, beef or chicken, 66
Sea bass baked in banana leaf 91

Soup:
beef, 72
chicken, 80
mutton (variation), 72
noodle, with meatballs 73
sour vegetable, 108
spinach, 110
with prawns (variation) 110
Soy sauce:
beef in, 71
chili, 42
fish in, 89
lamb in (variation), 76
pork fillet in, 76
sweet chili (variation), 42
sweet (kecap manis), 34
tofu in, 117
Soya bean cake, fried, 120
Soya beans 118
Spare ribs, barbecued, 79
Spinach soup 110: with prawns
(variation) 110
Spring rolls, Indonesian, 107
Squid: 48
sambal, fried, 48
curried, 60
fried, in batter (variation) 86
Stir-fried vegetables 102
Sweet chili-soy sauce (variation) 42
Sweet potato in coconut milk 130
Sweet-and-sour:
fish 90
pork 76
prawn (variation) 90
prawn sambal (variation) 51
tempeh (variation) 120
tofu (variation) 117

Tempeh:
with bean sprouts (variation) 120
sweet-and-sour (variation), 120
Terasi 96
Tofu:
with bean sprouts 118
curried noodles with (variation), 59
with peanut sauce 116
in soy sauce 117
sweet-and-sour (variation), 117

Vegetable:
salad with coconut 100
soup, sour, 108
mixed, curry 62
Vegetables:
in coconut milk 110
with peanut sauce 98

TIME
LIFE
BOOKS

Cover: Mackerel are marinated in a mixture of red chili peppers, garlic, sweet soy sauce, sugar and lemon juice, wrapped individually in pieces of banana leaf (*recipe, page 89*) and baked in the oven. The parcels make a striking and colourful main course when served with yellow rice topped with crispy fried onion rings (*recipe, page 28*) and hot chili *sambal ulek* (*recipe, page 42*).

TIME-LIFE BOOKS

COOKERY AROUND THE WORLD
English edition staff for *Indonesia*
Editorial: Ilse Gray, Luci Collings, Kate Cann, Charlotte Powell
Designer: Dawn McGinn
Production: Emma Wishart, Justina Cox
Technical Consultant: Michael A. Barnes

English translation by Isabel Varea for Ros Schwartz Translations, London

Published originally under the title *Küchen der Welt: Indonesien* by Gräfe und Unzer Verlag GmbH, Munich
© 1994 Gräfe und Unzer Verlag GmbH, Munich

This edition published by Time-Life Books B.V. Amsterdam
Authorized English language edition
© 1994 Time-Life Books B.V.
First English language printing 1994

ISBN 0 7054 1202 4

GRÄFE UND UNZER

EDITORS: Dr. Stephanie von Werz-Kovacs and Birgit Rademacker
Sub-Editor: Monika Arndt
Designer: Konstantin Kern
Recipes tested by: Monika Arndt
Production: Dr Helmut Neuberger & Karl Schaumann GmbH, Heimstetten
Cartography: Huber, Munich

Kusuma Widjaya was born in Jakarta and grew up in Java. Today, he is the owner of a hotel-restaurant on Bali specializing in local cuisine. This book combines classic Indonesian recipes with his own particular favourites.

Roland Marske, a freelance journalist and photographer living in Berlin, has travelled extensively in Africa and Asia. It was on one of these trips that he fulfilled an ambition to work on a cookery book with his friend Kusuma Widjaya.

Foodphotography Eising. Pete A. Eising and Susanne Eising specialize in food and drink photography and work closely with a food photography agency operating in Germany and Switzerland. As well as cookery publishers, their clients include advertising agencies, newspapers and magazines. The food and props stylist on this volume was Martina Görlach.

Heike Czygan, an illustrator and graphic artist with a leading Munich publishing house, has always been fascinated by Asia, especially Indonesia. Her illustrations, incorporating mythological motifs and images from shadow plays, reflect her love of decorative art.

Picture Credits

Colour illustrations: Heike Czygan

All photographs by Foodphotography Eising unless indicated below:

Cover: Graham Kirk, London. 4, top left (*stupas*—buildings housing sacred Buddhist relics—on the upper terraces of the temple at Borobudur, Java): Roland Marske, Berlin. 4, bottom left (sailing ships at the old Dutch port, Jakarta); bottom right (traditional wooden houses on Samosir, Lake Toba, northern Sumatra): Thomas Stankiewitz, Munich. 4, top right (the *kechak*, or monkey dance, Bali); 5, centre (boy with fighting cock, Lombok): Friedrich Stark, Dortmund. 8-9 (rice terraces and palm trees, Bali): Otto Sadler. 10, 11: Thomas Stankiewitz, Munich. 12, top: Freidrich Stark, Dortmund; bottom: Rüdiger Siebert, Weilerswist-Metternich. 13: Friedrich Stark, Dortmund. 14 (2), 15, bottom: Thomas Stankiewitz, Munich. 15, top, 16, bottom: Roland Marske, Berlin. 16, top: Silvestris Fotoservice, Kastl/Heiner Heine. 17: Friedrich Stark, Dortmund. 18: Roland Marske, Berlin. 19, top: Friedrich Stark, Dortmund; bottom: Roland Marske, Berlin. 20, top: Rüdiger Siebert, Weilerswist-Metternich; bottom: Roland Marske, Berlin. 21, 22: Roland Marske, Berlin. 23: Friedrich Stark, Dortmund. 24-5: Thomas Stankiewitz, Munich. 25, 31: Roland Marske, Berlin. 136: Otto Sadler.

The authors would like to thank the following for kindly providing accessories:
Sarong-Julius Gebhart, Indonesian Textiles, Munich
Artasia, Kunst-Handwerk-Wohnen, Munich
Caravanserai, Munich

Colour reproduction by Fotolito Longo, Bolzano, Italy
Typeset by A. J. Latham Limited, Dunstable, Bedfordshire, England
Printed and bound by Mondadori, Verona, Italy

2 3 4 5 6 7 8 9 10 11 12 13 14 15 16 17 18 19 20 21 22 23 24 25 26 27 28 29 30